NETWORKING HACKING

2 Books in 1:

Networking for Beginners,

Hacking with Kali Linux

By Dylan Mach

Networking for Beginners

Easy Guide to Learn Basic/Advanced Computer Network, Hardware, Wireless, and Cabling. LTE, Internet, and Cyber Security

By Dylan Mach

2

Table of Contents

3

Introduction

Congratulations on downloading Networking for Beginners, and thank you for doing so. The world is becoming digital, and everyone has to keep up with the constant emerging technologies. However, you can't involve in any type of technology without understanding the basics at first. That is, you have to initially learn the principles of different computer components before sinking deeper into complex activities such as computer programming and more.

The following chapters will discuss all you need to know about networking in the computing world essential for those who are venturing into the industry. Some may have limited knowledge about networking, but you are likely to become a pro soon when using this guide. Therefore, you will learn about different protocols used in networking as well as interconnection and the internet, among others. There are fundamental concepts in networking and may also include other forms of operations related to computer networks.

That said, you will learn about computer networking and understand how the modern telecommunication network facilitates the sharing of resources among machines. Networking is a fundamental field of computer study which allows for computers to become interconnected globally. Also, you will learn about machine learning as a form of algorithms and statistical methods of how machines acquire an ability to perform a given task. Machine learning is a broad topic but essential for beginners, especially when they want to learn about how computers are capable of making decisions on situations like humans.

There are plenty of books on this subject on the market, thanks again for choosing this one! Every effort was made to ensure it is full of as much useful information as possible. Please enjoy!

Chapter 1: Introduction to Machine Learning and Computer Networking

Machine learning and computer networking is both an essential field of study in computing but accompany different concepts. That is, they are topics that represent a similar study area on the contrary cover various sections of computer systems. In this case, machine learning entails computer algorithms and statistical models which facilitate the process of machine learning on data fed, the identity of suitable patterns, and the selection of the most favorable outcome. On the other hand, computer networking deals with the connections and interconnection of different computers globally, therefore, enabling data sharing, resource management, and user applications.

Computer Networking

Computer networking is the computing knowledge of studying and analyzing the communications techniques of computing devices or systems connected or interconnected together to exchange information or resources. A computer network is therefore defined as a group of computers allied together to communicate and share data and resources. Networking in computers solely depends on theoretical and practical applications of computer engineering, sciences, and telecommunication and information technologies. As to build computer networking between machines, an individual is required to have a router, network card, and specific protocols.

History of Computer Networks

Computer networking began during the rise of computers in the 1950s but utilized closed network systems used by the military. Unlike the modern networking systems, the late 1950s saw the use of military radars, which transitioned into MOS transistors consisting of transceivers, routers telecommunication circuits, and base station modules. Different developers proposed various forms of computer networking, including the introduction of a telephone switch in 1965 by the Western Electric. The first critical progress of computer networks began in the 1970s, which saw multiple modifications of devices used today to promote networking. One of them includes the Xerox PARC, which refers to the use of Ethernet, the X.25 used expanding IP network coverage and the creation of a host. From the supply of 50kb/s circuit in 1969 to the current 10mb/s to 100mb/s, the networking industry has undergone significant changes. However, the improvement is predicted to increase in the future, seeing the fastest modes of networks emerge, therefore building the computer networking sector. Besides, the higher speeds of the system have already been experienced with 2018. And this is because of the introduction of rates of up to 400 GB/s through the use of Ethernet fiber cables.

Components of Computer Networking

Routers

A router is the most common network device which forwards

data packets in computer networks with a primary function of directing traffic on the internet. The packets such as web pages are transmitted from one router to another comprising of an internetwork while waiting to reach a desirable node destination. Routers are commonly used in homes and small networks and perform using network cables rather than installed drivers and connected to the computers by use of USBs or specific wires.

Routers may either be wireless or consist of cables linked by ports to allow for devices to connect to the internet. They usually linked to the modem, for instance, fiber and DSL, or WAN ports via network cables to facilitate the connection. Based on your desirable network link, your network speed will vary, with some regulating the rate you receive per individual router. Besides, routers may follow specific IP addresses depending on the internet connection, with the private addresses being the primary gateway default one for different devices in the network. Multiple links to one router, including both wireless and wired devices, enable each one to communicate freely, such as the sharing of a printer.

Network Interface Card

A network card is an electronic device that connects one computer to a network, usually to a Local Area Network (LAN). Most modern computers have an embedded network interface card in the motherboard instead of having an external chip to connect a network. These cards are critical when the computer exchanges data with the computer network using a given protocol such as CSMA/CD. Previous versions of network cards used included protocols such as ARCNET incorporated in 1977, but today most computers use Ethernet. The use of Ethernet network cards has been the most common with the revolution of computer networking being witnessed each year.

Internet speeds often vary on network interface cards based on the protocol standards supported. The previous Ethernet cards supported up to 10mb/s with the current adapters supporting from 100mb/s up to 1000mb/s. Network cards do not necessarily support wireless connections, but routers also contain these cards, which determines the speeds for a given computer network. The same has been projected to increase in the near future with the use of Ethernet network cards. In this case, speeds are to grow in the coming years, with rates tripling the current figure. This is attributed to the expansion of usage of computer networking across different platforms, both in small enterprises to commercial use over the years.

Protocols

Computer networking also comprises connection protocols that consist of rules for two or more systems to exchange data.

Other than regulations, protocols also include syntaxes, communications synchronization, and semantics, as well as error recovery techniques, use in both hardware and software of computer connection. In other words, protocols are a set of rules which connect the server to the routers regardless of the variations in infrastructure, designs, and standards. As to exchange information, both parties much adhere to accept the protocols built in the hardware, software, or both.

Networking protocols usually accompany similar languages for the devices to facilitate the interaction between the two computers in the exchange of information. Network protocols typically utilize the Open Systems Interconnection (OSI) model used to break down the complicated process to readily defined functions and operations. There are multiple protocols used in computer networking, Transmission Control Protocol (TCP), User Datagram Protocol (UDP), Internal Protocol (IP), Hypertext Transfer Protocol (HTTP), and File Transfer Protocol (FTP), among others.

Types of Computer Networks

Local Area Network (LAN)

Local Area Network, commonly referred by its abbreviation, LAN, is a group of computer systems using and sharing a particular internet connection within a given small area such as the office or residential building. The LAN connection is usually through a communication medium, for instance, coaxial cables used by two or more personal computers. This type of computer network is often cheaper than other types and accessed by those within the area and uses hardware such as adapters and Ethernet cables. Transfer of data is commonly extremely fast with considerably higher security.

The connection only supports those within the area, and anyone outside tends to lack the transmission of information.

Personal Area Network (PAN)

This is a type of private network arranged within an area of 10 meters and often for personal use with devices within a given range. Personal Area Network was first researched and introduced by Thomas Zimmerman, who established that an individual could create a connection with communities with devices within 30 feet. Both wired and wireless PAN can be used in this type to connect to devices around the source. The source more so may generate from media players, laptops, and mobile phones. Wireless is usually connected using hotspots, Bluetooth, and Wi-Fi connected to devices within a given range. Wired PAN is connected by USB cables to facilitate the connection of a given network. Personal Area Network always moves with the person and can include offline systems and uses to connect devices using a VPN in small home networks.

Metropolitan Area Network (MAN)

Metropolitan Area Network is computer network which covers a wide range of a geographical area by interconnecting several LAN connections. This type of computer network is often used by government agencies to connect to different federal facilities as well as their citizens and private organizations. Some of the protocols in MAN include ISDN, Frame Relay, and OC-3, among others, which connect to different LANs through an exchange line. This form of a computer network is used in larger areas than that of LAN and such as airline reservations, military communication, colleges, and between banks.

Wide Area Network (WAN)

Wide Area Network is extended computer network coverage over a large geographical area such as between states or countries. It is quite extensive than LAN and WAN and not limited to one domain but covers an entirely larger area by use of satellite connections or fiber optic cables. WAN is the largest of all computer networks in the world and used in businesses, government operations, and educational purposes. Some of the advantages of WAN include centralized data, fast message transfer, coverage of a full geographical area, higher bandwidth, and supports global businesses. On the other hand, WAN can become disadvantageous in the case of a security breach; it demands a firewall and rigid antiviruses, expensive setup costs, and difficulty fixing problems due to its more comprehensive coverage.

Machine Learning

As mentioned, machine learning is the method of data analysis by computers where algorithms and statistical models play a role for machines to learn from data and patterns and then make decisions without human interactions. Since its incorporation in the late 1950s, machine learning has gained popularity and become a vast topic in computing. It is a branch of artificial intelligence enabling computers to provide analytical information about the future with limited human interaction. Machine learning can, therefore, be learned in different ways depending on the part an individual chooses to follow.

The idea of machine learning takes the form of the human brain, including the neurons and how they facilitate the assimilation of information, thinking, and making decisions. When the concept was first introduced to computers in 1943, it focused on neural networks where machines became capable of learning on their own, depending on the information fed. That is, machines were able to observe, learn, understand, analyze, and make decisions based on the event without depending on individual instructions. However, the slow development of computers at the time increased the challenges of machine learning when compared to the current days.

As humans have the ability to develop and expand their knowledge about an event or something they first or learn, the same technique, therefore, facilitate machine learning. Besides, humans depend on networks of neurons in the brain, and computers utilize a similar pattern. As such, machine work with the same technique, therefore, can manage to make decisions and conclusions without any human interaction. However, the decisions made by computers are widely based on mathematical and algorithms that have expanded to make them predict the outcome of things that haven't happened yet. Currently, different methods have been used, therefore enabling computers to learn specific information; therefore, be able to provide predictions, conclusions, and decisions based on specific datasets.

Machine Learning Vs. Computer Programming

Machine learning has been widely confused with computer language programming, which in this case, has significant dissimilarities. As defined, machine learning is all about the machine receiving specific data sets, selecting the most reliable algorithm, learn and determine the outcome without any human interaction. It, therefore, has limited interaction, especially when analysis the information, learning, and making positive outcomes. On the contrary, computer programming requires human interaction who first selects datasets to use and writing them in the machine. The codes are then executed to create a specific program, which is, therefore, the outcome. In programming, machines rarely learn but generated results based on the instructions provided by humans.

General Steps in Machine Learning

Collection and Preparation of Data

Humans can never learn and have knowledge about something without having an interaction or understanding the basics. Similarly, machines face a similar challenge, as they also have to gain access to relevant information about something before learning in detail about it. As such, the first step in machine learning is to collect the necessary data and prepare it in a way that fits a given criterion. The collection comprises of gaining access to specific details about a given element and begin having an understanding about it. The computer then prepares the system to internalize the information before providing the needed knowledge.

Selection of Instructing Models

Humans also undergo trial and error in order to come up with an effective solution to a problem at hand. Machine learning also creates multiple models based on the instructions fed to provide the most suitable model, which can solve a given problem. In this case, the computer uses algorithms which have been modified differently since their incorporation. Over the years, more models have been developed with the objective of making machines more specific in some regions of specialization. In this step, computers, therefore, select the most desirable model that best suits a given dataset and train itself through learning more about the information at hand. This ensures that the information fed and the outcomes are more likely to become beneficial and provide the intended solution.

Evaluation of Models

The last step is now to put the model selected into practice by trying to figure out if the model which enables the machine to learn and make decisions without human interaction. Machines readily learn from the information fed and create patterns and work like how we behave on newfound knowledge in our minds. That is, when supplied with well-tested details, the machine will offer excellent results with inadequate tests leading to vogue and harmful outcomes. In this step, you need to feed the computer with the relevant models and data which provide an algorithm where the machine will follow and deliver effective results. Therefore, test the data and model, which provides certainty of delivering exceptional results.

Types of Machine Learning Algorithms

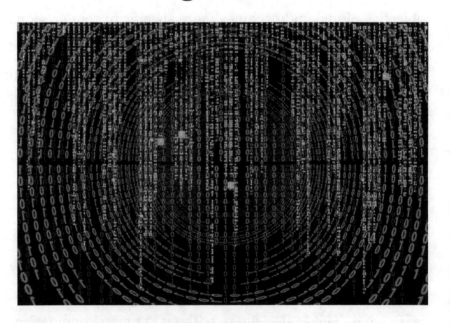

Supervised Algorithms

As mentioned, machine learning comprises of multiple types depending on how the data fed is to yield the outcome. One of the models is the supervised algorithm, where the datasets undergo a given set of parameters, which in turn determine the outcome. The machine initially specifies the data into labels as well as the training data included. In this case, the data is initially tested to ascertain its outcome, therefore, controlling the outcome. This type of algorithm usually has a manageable as a result is generally intended. Supervised algorithms are further subdivided into classification and regression algorithms.

The classification algorithm uses the K-Nearest Neighbor classification algorithm, which is responsible for sorting data into individual labels. The data is classified depending on the similarities between variables or the information inputted in the machine. On the other hand, regression algorithms focus on mathematical relationships and the dependency of variables. That is, it provides an immediate analysis of numerical datasets with similarities essential for predicting the future. The regression algorithm includes two forms depending on the information fed, linear, and logistic regression models.

Unsupervised Algorithms

This is the opposite of supervised algorithms and consists of unlabeled datasets, which in most cases, the results are undetermined. The unsupervised algorithm is classified into

K-means clustering, recurrent, and artificial neural network. The artificial neural networks resemble the brain neurons, which are connected and interconnected to enhance learning, thinking, and making decisions without any interventions. K-means clustering entails the grouping of similar data into clusters to promote learning in machines. While recurrent neural networks use the memory in the nodes of computer neurons to analyze sequential information for the benefit of encouraging decision making in devices.

Reinforcement Algorithms

Reinforcement algorithms are where the machines determine specific information is the datasets within particular contexts. As one of the types of machine learning algorithms, reinforcement models are the most beneficial as learning of specific datasets leads to the maximization of the outcome. However, if the wrong dataset is fed into the machine, it may result in extensive punishments or other related dangers. But when using the right parameters, the device will make the needed corrections and yield positive results. Besides, this type of machine learning algorithm enables you to quickly make corrections, modifications, or change the outcome if you feel it may become undesirable in the future.

Applications of Machine Learning

Since the introduction of machine learning in the computing industry, different sectors have benefited significantly in their operations. More so, it has popularity between developers as well as other users, making it applicable in different areas. In this case, the applications of machine learning range from small scale technological businesses to commercial use. One of the common areas includes social media such as Facebook and Twitter used for sentimental analysis, spam filtering, facial recognition, among others. It is also applied in the e-commerce sector to display items that are mostly searched by specific clients. Machine learning is also used in areas such as transport, health, trading, visual assistance, and financial services.

Chapter 2: Properties of a Computer Network

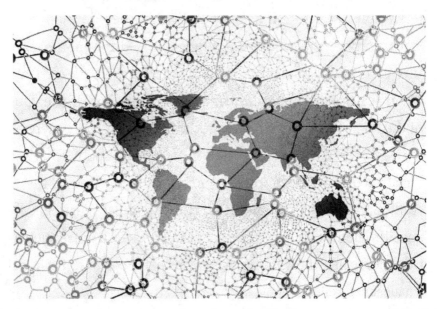

A computer network is defined as a digital telecommunications network that allows resources to be shared between nodes. A telecommunication network is a number of terminal nodes having connected links that would enable telecommunication between some terminals. Transmission links in the network act as a connection between nodes. Telecommunications network allows for interactions and transfer of information over long distances. Computer network involves a connection between computer systems and computer hardware devices via communication channels. The communication channels enable communication and sharing of resources amongst many users. The connections between nodes are referred to as data links. The establishment of the data links is usually from cable media, including optic cables or wires, and wireless media, including Wi-Fi.

Network nodes are the network computer devices originating, routing, and terminating the data. Typically, the nodes are identified through network addresses, and generally include elements such as phones, personal computers, networking hardware, and servers. The devices are easily networked together as long as one of the tools has the ability to exchange information with the other devices. The devices can either have or not have a direct connection with each other.

A wide range of services and applications are supported by computer networks. Some of them include accessing the digital audio, digital video, World Wide Web, the common use of storage servers, and applications, fax machines, and printers. It may also include the use of instant messaging and e-mail applications. Computer networks differ from other telecommunication networks because of the transmitting mediums they use in carrying their signals, protocols used in organizing network traffic, size of the networks, the mechanism in controlling traffic, organizational intent, and topology. One of the most common computer networks is the Internet.

Computer networks have been in existence since the late

1950s. During this time, computer networks involved the Semi-Automatic Ground Environment. The SAGE was a radar system used by the U.S military. A reorganization was later planned in 1959. It was based on the network of the OGAS, which were computing center networks. The MOS transistor was also invented in 1959 at Bell Labs by Dawon Kahng, and Mohamed Atalla. The conductor was one of the significant steps towards computer network communication infrastructure. It included base station modules, routers, memory chips, telecommunication circuits, microprocessors, transceivers, and RF power amplifiers.

SABRE a system in the commercial airline reservation, managed to go online with two mainframes that were connected together in 1960. The intergalactic computer network was later invented in 1963. It allowed for general communications amongst many computer users. In 1964, some researchers came up with an operation where a computer was used in routing and managing connections between telephones.

The concept of packet switching was developed all through the 1960s. It allowed for information to be transferred among computers through a network. A telephone was also used in implementing the precise control of computers. A paper was later published on Wide Area Network that allowed computers to share time.

French CYCLADES hosts were developed by 1973. The hosts

had the responsibility to deliver data instead of centralizing services on the network reliably. A formal memo was written in the same year with a description of Ethernet. Ethernet is one of the most common networking systems used in the world today. Robert Metcalfe worked from 1979 in a bid to make Ethernet open standard. Ethernet continued being upgraded to a 10Mbit/s protocol in the 1980s.

By 1995, Ethernet was supporting gigabit speeds. It has the capability of having a transmission speed of up to 400Gbit/s as recorded in 2018. The continued use of Ethernet results from its capacity to adapt and to scale easily.

Properties of Computer Network

Computer networking is considered a subdivision of

electronics engineering, computer engineering, computer science, electrical engineering, information technology, or telecommunications. This is because the practical and theoretical computer networking relies on have close relations to the fields.

Computer networks allow for efficient interpersonal communication between users. They can effectively communicate through video telephone calls, telephone, online chats, instant messaging, video conferencing, and e-mails. It also allows for network and computing resources sharing among users. Accessing and using resources is made easier through the devices on the network. Users can, for instance, share printers and storage devices together. Data, files, and other forms of information can also be shared effectively using computer networks.

Uses of Computer Networks

If it were not beneficial, people would not have considered creating a connection between computers through a network. There are numerous users of computer networks in the world today. They are used to benefit both individuals and companies in the long run.

Use in Business Applications

• Resource Sharing

The main goal of computer networks is ensuring the anything about a business is available to all those who take part. Computer networks allow for this access by making all equipment, data, and programs available to any person using the network. Any user can access the use of the computer network regardless of their physical location.

• Server-Client Model

In such a model, the information about a business is stored on servers, which are powerful computers. The servers are housed centrally, and a system administrator is used to maintain them. The business employees usually have clients, which are simple machines on their office desks. The server-client model allows for easier access to remote data and information by these employees.

• Communication-Medium

Employees in a business setting need to communicate on various issues affecting business operations regularly. Computer networks, therefore, offer a powerful medium for communication among the employees. Almost all companies have several computers with logged-in e-mails. Employees use these computers when on great deals of communicating on a daily basis. An employer can send a message, and everyone engaging in the business operations can easily receive it.

- ## eCommerce

One of the most significant targets of every business is the ability to do business with potential customers through the Internet. In the modern world, most customers prefer doing their shopping from home. Numerous ventures such as music vendors, books, and food stores have considered using computer networks to meet the needs of their customers.

- ## High Reliability because of Alternative Sources of Data

Computer networks provide higher reliability by providing numerous sources of data. This means that general files can be copied on many machines. When one of the machines is not available, another one can be used to access the same information. The concept of Reliability is significant in banking, military, nuclear reactor safety, and military. This is because such sectors require consistent operations, even when there are hardware and software failures.

- ## **Money-Saving**

Computer networking is a significant concept of the financial aspect for many companies and businesses. This is because it saves a considerable amount of money. Computer networks provide an option for using personal computers rather than mainframe computers that are quite expensive. Companies can effectively use the peer to peer model by networking all personal computers together. Everyone in the organization can access the network for many purposes, such as communication. The domain model offered by computer networks can help to provide security to the operations of an organization. Clients involved in the organization can access data and communicate with the organization through the server.

- ## **Computer Networks: Home Applications**

Home users also consider using computer networks for

various reasons. Some of these include:

Accessing remote information- People connect their devices for easier access to useful information.

Person-to- person communication- This communication includes sending e-mails or other forms of communication. Remote users are able to communicate with other people easily. They are able to see and hear from other people who are away from them without delays. Video-conferencing is one of the most popular person-to-person communication, is used in remote schools, or receiving medical opinions from medical practitioners who are distant. People also consider using computer networks to access information posted by worldwide newsgroups easily. Through these networks, people easily give their feedbacks regardless of their physical location.

Interactive Entertainment- Computer networks allow for easier access to videos on demand, multi-person simulation games, and participation of people in live television programs such as discussions, and quizzes. It is through these networks that people can feel the entertainment from the comfort of their homes. People also use computer networks as home applications for electronic commerce.

Computer Networks: Mobile Users

Mobile computers include personal digital assistants and notebooks. They are one of the segments in the computer industry growing at a very rapid rate. Owners of mobile computers usually possess desktop computers in their offices and prefer connecting them to their portable computers based at home. Computer networks allow for wireless connection to these devices, even when in an airplane or a car. One main reason why people connect to these mobile computers is to allow them to receive telephone calls and messages, send faxes, e-mails, access remote files, and surf through the web. People are able to do all this from any location away from their office.

More Information on Types of Computer Networks

Computer networks are basically used for numerous tasks in the world today. Some of the tasks include downloading attachments and printing documents. This is done by referring to several devices within a room and spreading them across the entire world. This can be defined based on their purpose or their size. Below are some of the common types of computer networks.

• Personal Area Network (PAN)

A personal area network is the most basic and smallest type of computer network. It is comprised of a computer(s), phones, tablets, printers, and a wireless modem. PAN revolves around a single person within a building. The networks are commonly used in residences and small offices. Their management is controlled by one organization or person from one device.

• Local Area Network (LAN)

Local area networks are popularly discussed by people in the world today. They are one of the most original, simplest, and common types of computer networks. They are used in connecting together several computers and devices of low voltage. The devices are usually within short distances, such as different rooms within a building or several buildings close to each other. They help in sharing resources and information among the connected devices. LAN computer networks are commonly used by enterprises. They are easily manageable and maintainable.

• Wireless Local Area Network (WLAN)

WLAN networks function in a similar way as the LAN networks. The networks use wireless network technology. Some of them include Wi-Fi. WLAN networks do not require devices to have physical cables when connecting to it.

• Campus Area Network

Campus area networks are quite larger than Local area networks but smaller than the metropolitan area networks.

CANs are commonly used in small businesses, universities, colleges, and large school districts. Campus area networks are spread across a number of buildings that are closer to each other. They allow any user in the different buildings to connect and share resources.

- ## Metropolitan Area Networks

Metropolitan networks are larger than the local area networks but smaller than the wide-area networks. They include the elements of both types of computer networks. MANS computer networks can spread on a whole geographical area such as a city or a town. The ownership and management of the computer network is usually under one company, such as a local council or by a single person such as the owner of a particular company.

- ## Wide Area Network

Wide area network is quite complex as compared to the local area network. WANs computer networks easily create connections with computers in wide distant locations. Low voltage devices, as well as computers, create a remote connection with each other. They do this through a single large network allowing communication even longer distances. WAN computer networks have different categories, with the Internet being the most basic type. The Internet allows for the connection of computers all over the globe. Numerous public and administration entities typically own WAN computer networks. This is possible due to its wider reach.

• Storage-Area Network (SAN)

SAN computer networks are of high-speed and significantly dedicated. They create connections between shared sources of storage devices and various servers. SAN networks do not rely on WAN and LAN. The computer networks typically removed the storage devices from the computer networks and put them on their high-performance networks. The computer networks are accessible similarly to drives attached to servers. Some of the types of Storage Area Networks include, unified SANs, and converged virtual SANs.

• System-Area Network

This type of computer network is quite new and is also abbreviated as SANs. The computer networks are basically used in defining relative local networks. The networks are designed high-speed connections in applications involving servers, processors, as well as storage area networks. Computers are connected to this type of network operating as single systems and offer very rapid speeds.

• Passive Optical Local Area Network (POLAN)

POLAN computer networks are used as a substitute for

traditional switch-based Ethernet LANs. The technology used in POLAN computer networks is added to structured cabling. The reason behind the integration is overcoming concerns on the support of traditional network applications, and Ethernet protocols. Optical splitters are used in POLAN to enhance the splitting of optical signals from a single strand. Single-mode-mode optical fibers are transformed into numerous signals that serve devices and users.

• Enterprise Private Network (EPN)

Enterprise private Networks are owned by businesses that typically build them. Businesses prefer this type of computer networks as a way of securing the connection between various locations that share the network.

• Virtual Private Network (VPN)

The extension of a private network all over the Internet is made possible by the use of Virtual Private Network. Sending and receiving information and data between connected devices is also made possible by the VPNs computer networks. The process is also possible when users are using devices that are not directly connected. Access to remote private networks is also made possible through a connection referred to as point-to-point.

Basic Elements of Computer Networks

Computer Networks comprise of systems through which a connection is created between numerous nodes. The links help them to share resources and information. Computer network elements are the fundamental objects used in computer networks. Basically, there are four significant elements of computer networking. These include computers, transmission medium, protocols, and network software. For a computer network to successfully function, all the elements have to work in coordination.

- ## Computers

Computers are digital devices that can accept input in the form of data, process it through the use of data structures, and predefined algorithms, performing tasks in the form of output. The process can be defined as transforming raw data into useful information. The output provided includes performing several physical tasks as well as storing data, transforming it as well as retrieving it when in need. The network is created by computers to allow for leveraging of distributed models of programming and interchanging data to allow for equivalent processing.

- ## Transmission Medium

The transmission medium is the path through which users send data from one place to a new place. When representing data, computers and telecommunication devices make use of signals. The transmission of the signals from one device to the other is generally through electromagnetic energy. They are transmitted through air, vacuums, and different modes from the sender to the receiver. There are two types of transmission mediums. The Guided or Wired transmission mediums include optical fiber cables, twisted pair cable, and coaxial cables. The Unguided or Wireless transmission mediums include infrared, radio waves, and microwaves.

• **Protocols**

Protocols are the defined conventions and rules guiding communication between computer network devices. Computer network protocols consist of device mechanisms used in identifying and making connections between each other. Formality rules are used in specifying the method of packaging data in the form of received and sent messages. There are three types of protocols. The internet protocols, wireless network protocols, and network routing protocols.

Internet protocols are the rules set to govern the format of sending data through the Internet or over another network. They are the standards used to address and route data on the Internet. The internet protocols deliver packets from the host to a destination host entirely depending on the addresses on the headers of the packages. Wireless network protocols involve a collection of wireless devices and laptops engaging in communication through radio waves. Computer network routing protocols, on the other hand, are used in specifying methods through which routers are communicating with each other. They do this through the distribution of information, enabling them to choose routes among nodes within computer networks. Routing algorithms are used when determining particular routes of choice. Computer network routing protocols are capable of adjusting dynamically to evolving conditions, including disabled computers, and data lines.

- ## Network Software

Computer networks use network software as foundation elements for all networks. Network software assists administrators in deploying, managing, and monitoring any network. Numerous traditional networks consist of special hardware, including switches and routers that integrate networking software in the combination. Networking software consists of a wide range of software applied in designing, implementing, operating, and monitoring computer networks. Most traditional computer networks were based on hardware but embedded in the software. Defined Networking, that was software like emerged and led to the separation of software from hardware. This separation made network software much adaptable to the evolving nature of computer networks.

Choosing a Suitable Computer Network

There are factors that one should consider when selecting a computer network type for an organization. These factors include:

The Organization- One should consider finding out the sector of the economy that the organization operates, what the organization is providing, the number of people employed in the organization, as well as the jobs they are working on.

Existing Systems- It is essential to check on the existing computer network components, the network operating system, network architecture, transmission medium, and topology.

Number of Users- Prior to choosing a computer network for an organization, it is crucial to check on the number of users. This is because organizations tend to have users working on separate as well as shared workstations.

Functionality- Consider checking on tasks undertaken by the network users as well as software applications being used in carrying out the tasks.

Budget- Consider choosing a computer network operator that is within your budget. This helps to guarantee successful implementation and maintenance of the network.

Chapter 3: Easy Guide to Learn Basic Computer Network

This article discusses the basic components of computer networking and the easy ways you can learn them. It also extensively discusses the advanced features of computer networking as well as how you can learn and apply them. Read on to find out!

Computer Networking has been in existence for quite some time now, and with time, technology has become quicker and more affordable. These networks are a build-up of various devices and components, including computers, routers, and switches, which are linked together by wireless signals or cables. Learning how these networks and connections are assembled is very essential in creating a network that can be used for many purposes.

In the quest of breaking this giant of a topic down, let us start by discussing the essential components of any computer network.

The Important Components of a Computer Network

This is the first thing you need to look at when learning computer networks. Any computer network is made up of four very important components: Media, Networking Devices, Protocols, and End Devices. Let us discuss each of these essential components.

• The End Devices

This is a kind of device that either sends or receives a set of data or information within a particular network. End devices can be laptops, smartphones, PC, or any kind of machine with the capabilities of receiving or sending the set of data within the connected network. For your information, you will need a minimum of two devices to build a network.

There are two types of end devices: client end devices and the server end devices. The server end device is responsible for providing service or data. On the other hand, the client end device is one which is responsible for receiving the data offered from the former (the server end device).

• The Media

This is a very important component of the computer network that provides connectivity and linkage for the end devices. End devices are not able to exchange services or data unless they are connected through any kind of media. As of today, there exist mainly two categories or types of media: the wired media and the wireless media.

Radio signals are mainly applied in transferring data and information between the end devices when using Wireless Media. In wired media, however, cables are used instead.

The above-mentioned types of media are further subdivided into various subtypes depending on factors like the data transfer speed, length, frequency band, among others. The subtypes are commonly referred to as media standards. The media standards that are popular and widely applied are the IEEE802.11 (also known as Wi-Fi standards) and the Ethernet.

The two media standards play different essential roles. The Ethernet is responsible for defining standards for wired media while the IEEE802.11 plays a role in defining standards for wireless media.

• The Protocols

Just like the previous two, this is a very important component

49

of a computer network. Protocols are responsible for the communication between the involved end devices; they could be two or more. A protocol is defined as a group of rules that highlights and specifies the standards for a specific or all the stages of communication.

Below are some known roles played by protocols.

- o Starting and ending the communication process.
- o Doing Encryption and compressions before transferring any data.
- o Packaging data in such a format that it is able to travel within a network.
- o Establishing and providing logical addresses
- o Carrying out error correction processes
- o Performing media authentication

Two popular models of networking describe the functionalities of most common protocols: TCP/IP model and the OSI reference model. These models categorize the entire process of communication into logical layers. They further explain how each protocol works in every layer, which enables the process of communication.

• The Networking Device

This is an essential component of computer networking that works in between the end devices. It is responsible for controlling the smooth flow of data. Depending on its functionality, networking devices are categorized into three different types; the forwarding device, the connecting device, and lastly, the securing device. Below, we discuss the functionality of each of the mentioned devices.

- o **Connecting Device:** It is responsible for connecting two or more types of protocols and media. In situations where two end devices are situated in different geographical networks or connected via a distinct type of media, they will require a connecting hatchet to carry out data exchange. This functionality can be provided through Multilayer and Router switch.

- o **Securing Device**: This device is responsible for securing data from any unauthorized access. The securing device does security checks basing on the predefined rules whenever it receives a data packet. It then forwards it or rejects it based on the decision made. Some of the commonly known devices that perform these functions are NAT and Firewall.

- o **Forwarding Device:** This is a device responsible for forwarding data. It has multiple sections and ports mainly used in connecting more two or more end devices in just one network. The two commonly known devices for these functions are Hub, Ethernet, and Bridge switches.

Having learned about the four essential components of a computer network, we next discuss other features that are much significance in computer networking.

Routers, switches, and wireless access points play a very significant role in computer networks. Below, discuss how this is done.

• **Switches**

These are the basic requirement for the majority of business networks. A switch, as most of us know, acts as controller linking printers, computers and servers within a computer network.

They enable the devices within a network to establish communication within themselves as wells as building a network commonly shared resources. Switches save a lot of money through resource allocation and sharing. They also increase the rate of productivity. There exist two commonly known types of switches in computer networking; managed switches and unmanaged switches.

An unmanaged type of switch is that which is able to work outside the box and can not be configured. The network equipment established at home specifically offers unmanaged switches. On the other hand, a managed switch is that which can be configured. It gives you the capability to adjust and monitor the progress of network traffic. It, therefore, gives you more control over the entire networking process.

• **Routers**

These are essential components that are responsible for

connecting multiple sets of networks. They are also tasked with connecting the computers within a given network to a functioning Internet. They make it possible for all the networked devices or computers to share one Internet connection, which in the long run, saves you money.

Routers act as dispatchers. They analyze the data sent across a given network, find the quickest route data can travel and sends it that way.

They are able to link your business to the outside world, protect the vital information from threats, and even make decisions on the computers that are eligible to receive more attention over others.

Apart from the known networking roles they play, routers are equipped with a set of more features that make the networking process even easier and safer. Basing on the needs you have, for instance, you can buy a router with a virtual private network commonly known as VPN, a firewall, or the Internet Protocol, which is commonly known as IP.

• The Access Points

This is another essential aspect of a computer network that enables the devices to link to the network (a wireless network) without using cables. Wireless networks make it easier to invite fresh devices on online networks and give a flexible form of assistance to remote workers.

They act as amplifiers for your computer network. While

routers provide bandwidth, the access point broadens the provided bandwidth in ways that networks are able to provide support to a good number of devices. These devices can then access the Internet from locations far away from where the router is located.

What you should know, however, is that the access points don't just extend the Wi-Fi reach. It also provides essential information about devices connected to the network; it also gives proactive safety measures and plays other critical functions.

Additionally, the access points can support various IEEE standards. Every standard, as we have discussed earlier, is an assortment that has been ratified over a period of time. Such standards run on a set of different frequencies, produce a different set of bandwidth and provide the help needed from a host of deferent channels.

• **Wireless Networks**

When creating a wireless network, you have the option to choose between four different types of deployment. Every form of deployment has characteristics that work better in various solution searching missions.

     o **Cisco Mobility Express:** Cisco mobility is a simple, best performing wireless solution that is aimed at helping medium or small-sized companies. It is equipped with complete features of cisco that usually preconfigured the best practices of Cisco advance. The defaults created will enable the fast and effortless deployment of Wi-Fi that can operate in a few minutes. This is the most recommended module, especially for small computer networking businesses.

o **The Centralized Deployment:** The commonly known type of computer networking system is centralized deployment. They are basically used in learning institutions where structures are located closer together. This kind of deployment involves a wireless network that eases upgrades and ensures the advanced functionality of wireless networks. The controllers of these devices are installed based on-premises and set up in mostly in a central location.

o **The Converged Deployment:** This kind of deployment is mostly done in small proximity establishments like small campuses or branch offices. That provides a set of consistency in both wired and wireless connections. The convergent deployment redirects the wired and wireless connections on a single network and then carries out the double role of the switch and as the wifeless controller.

o **The Cloud-Based Deployment:** This deployment method puts into use the cloud to run the devices dispatched on-site at different locations. This kind of solution needs a Cisco Meraki cloud-managed gadget that gives a full view of a computer network through visible dashboards.

The Classification of Computer Network

Having learned about the essential details of a computer network, it is time we discussed the classification of computer networks. This is a very important topic for anyone in quest of learning computer networking.

Computer networks are categorized based on various factors, namely: the geographical location, the relationship between devices, and the access types.

Let us look at each criterion and find out the credentials in detail.

Basing on Geographical Location

When using the geographical coverage criteria, the network

device is subdivided into three different types: MAN, WAN, and LAN. The network spread in small, medium, and much wider geographical areas are referred to as the WAN, LAN, and MAN work networks in that order.

Based on the Access Type

When basing on allowing different users to have access to the network resources, the network can be grouped into three different types: Intranet, Extranet, and lastly, the Internet.

Intranet refers to any private network. In this kind of network, users from outside do not have access to provided network resources.

An extranet is almost similar to an intranet as it is a private network. In this network, however, external users are allowed access to a small portion of internet resources after proper scrutiny and authorization.

The Internet, on the other hand, is a public network. Any individual or user can have access to it provided they have devices that can access it.

Basing on Relationships between End Devices

In this criteria, the Internet is broken down into two sets: the clients/server network and the peer to peer network. In the peer to peer network, the available end devices all have fair, equal rights. In the client/server network, however, the decision on which client will receive what rights lie in the hands of the server.

Next, we look at the various types of computer networks. This is also a very important area where, as a person learning computer networking, you need to know.

Computer networks are categorized by their size. There are mainly four types of computer networks, namely; WAN (Wide Area Network), MAN(Metropolitan Area Network), PAN (Personal Area Network) and LAN (Local Area Network). Let us discuss each of these networks extensively and find out what they entail.

• **Local Area Network (LAN)**

LAN refers to a number of computers linked and connected to one another within a small space like a house or office. The Local Area Network is mainly used in the connection of two or more computers via a communication channel such as the coaxial cable and the twisted pair. LAN is cheaper because it is constructed with affordable hardware, including Ethernet cables, network adapters as well as hubs. Data is transferred quicker in LAN than any other network. The Local Area Network gives more secure network options.

• **The Personal Area Network (PAN)**

This is a type of network that is arranged around an individual, to be more specific, within ten meters. PAN is mainly used in connecting computer devices that mainly for personal use. Thomas Zimmerman, a research scientist, first brought the idea of Personal Area Network. This kind of network can cover an area of up to 30 feet. You can use personal computers to develop this kind of network. Such kinds of computers are mobile phones, laptops, desktops, play stations, and media players.

As of today, there exist two categories of Personal Area Network: Wired Personal Area Network and the Wireless Personal Area Network. The wireless one is developed by the use of wireless innovations like Bluetooth and Wi-Fi. This is usually a low range network.

The wired network, on the other hand, is built by the use of USB cables.

- ## Examples of PAN

    The Body Area Network: this is a kind of network that is moved along with a person. For instance, mobile networks are moved with an individual. Now suppose that the individual in possession of the mobile network establishes a connection and invites other devices to share the information and connection.

    Offline Networks: This kind of network can be built when just at home. It is specially designed to connect and link different devices, namely computers, printers, and radio sets. You, however, need to note that the devices are not connected to the Internet.

The Small Home Office: This kind of network is mainly used to link and connect a number of elements to the internet connection and a cooperate link through a VPN.

• The Metropolitan Area Network (MAN)

MAN is a kind of network that can cover a large geographical area by joining a different kind of local area network to create a larger network. The metropolitan area network is mainly used in government organizations as well as private companies to connect citizens. In this kind of network, there are several local area networks connected via a telephone line. Some of the commonly used protocols in metropolitan area networks are ATM, Frame Relay ADSL, among others. MAN has a wide coverage and range compared to the local land network.

• Uses of MAN

It is used in establishing communication between financial institutions like banks within a city.

MAN can be applied in the reservation of airlines.

Additionally, a metropolitan area network is used in learning institutions that are located within a city. It is also used in the creation of communication modules in the military.

• The Wide Area Network (WAN)

WAN is a kind of network that covers very large geographical locations and regions like countries or States. WAN is very big compared to the local area network. It is not pinned down to a single location but rather can be distributed over large areas through fiber optic cables or satellite links. For your information, the Internet is one of the best forms of WAN. The Wide Area Network is largely used in fields of education, business, and government.

• Examples of WAN

The mobile broadband: in this kind of network, the 4G network is popularly used across a country.

Last Mile Internet: This is the situation where a telecommunication company provides internet services to users in different locations by connecting their residences with fiber optic internet.

The Private Network: Banks provide a set of private networks that can connect up to forty-four offices. The private network is build using telephone lines usually provided by telecom companies in charge.

- ## Advantages of WAN

  Highlighted below are some of the advantages of WAN.

  The geographical coverage: WAN covers a larger geographical location than any other network. For instance, if a branch of a certain office is located in a different town or city, you can be connected to it through the Wide Area Network. The Internet gives a leeway through which you can be able to connect with a branch located in a different location.

  It offers Centralized Data: Data is centralized in Wide area networks. You, therefore, don't require to have emails or other back up systems.

  Wide Area Network has provided an updated file. Various software organizations have work done on live servers. This means that programmers are able to access updated files within a matter of seconds.

  WAN networks provide for the exchange of Messages where they are transferred in a fast way. You can see how this is applied in real life through web apps like Facebook and Skype, which allow you to communicate with loved ones.

  WAN enables the sharing of resources and software:

You are allowed to share software and a host of other resources like RAM when using the wide-area network.

Additionally, WAN enables you to do business in large, global regions.

Lastly, the wide-area network has higher bandwidth. It occurs If you decide to use lines that have been leased for your company when WAN gives you the highest bandwidth. Higher bandwidth is capable of increasing the rate of data transfer, which in return improves the productivity of your organization.

The Internetwork

This can be defined as a number of computer networks, WAN, or LANs that are linked using devices and configured by the basic addressing machine. The process of doing all this is referred to as interconnection. Having interconnections between commercial, public, and private computer networks can also be referred to as internetworking. Mostly, internetworking uses internet protocol. Open System Interconnection (OSI) is the model of reference used in internetworking.

Chapter 4: What Are the Basic Cybersecurity Fundamentals?

Cybersecurity is a popular name in the internet and other technological advancement areas. It has got many concerns recently due to the increased cyber threats and attacks. Simply because; more systems are being targeted using more sophisticated strategies in assaults. It is a menace that has an impact on small-scale and large-scale businesses, individuals, organizations, schools, workplaces, and so on. It is with great importance that we all have to understand cybersecurity and what measures we can invent to solve any threats and attacks. Recently, there has been growth in the use of mobile banking, social networking, and online shopping by individuals, businesses, organizations, or enterprises. As much as it is a convenient way of getting services, it can come with a lot of danger. Simply because all these services can be acquired online, and that is an excellent harbor of cybercriminals who are waiting to lay a trap on your system. To be on a safe side, you may need to have the basic knowledge of cybersecurity fundamentals.

What Is Cybersecurity?

It is the process of protecting programs, computer systems, networks, sensitive information, and software applications. It involves using several techniques, practices, and procedures against cyber-attacks, damage, or unauthorized access.
Cybersecurity is a vital aspect in any organization as it guarantees them the safety of their data. However, in some

cases, it tricky solving the cyber-attack menace due to inadequate systems, advanced threats, and attackers. Though, it does not mean it is entirely impossible to get the system going and protect your information at any cost. Let's have a look at some of these attacks and threats affecting information:

Botnets Attacks

Initially, botnets referred to as a network or group of devices connected on the same network to work together. However, this worked in the wrong way. Hackers and other cybercriminals have taken the objective of turning its primary function to create chaos. They do this by injecting malware or other malicious codes to disrupt its normal functioning. It happens due to stealing sensitive and confidential data or emails and also spreading spam emails. In most cases, these attacks are prone to large scale organizations that have a large volume of data at their disposal. These hackers take advantage and manipulate the system to their advantage and creating chaos within the organization.

Crypto-currency Hijacking

In recent times, there has been the use of digital currency and mining. It is so prevalent in the business world, and so is with cybercriminals. They are inventing new ways of using the crypto-currency mining for their convenience on a disruptive and harmful way. They use crypto hacking, a program that injected into the mining systems. It then silently accesses the CPU, GPU, and power resources of the affected system to mine for the crypto-currency inform of Monero coins. It is an advanced threat that gets the hacker using your resources such as the internet and electricity. The process in itself is complex and wears off your system comfortably and later affects its functionality. In most cases, the cryptocurrency traders and their investors are at significant risk.

Ransomware

It is a type of software encryption program file that uses a unique, robust encryption algorithm to encrypt data on a target system. This threat makes it hard to view any files on any application. The authors of this threat have a unique decryption key for the affected systems, which clears them using a remote server. In this case, the hackers involved in its creation will demand a ransom from the affected person to decrypt their data and save their systems. However, this does not guarantee you will have all your data back after paying the ransom.

Phishing

Here a typical kind of attack that involves sending spam

emails to people or organizations by imitating legitimate sources. Most of the emails sent through this fraudulent way tend to have secure attachments to confuse you into thinking they came from a real person. For instance, they have active job offers, invoices, offers, and promotions from reputable companies or organizations or can be an email from a higher official of the organization and a government official.

However, the main objective of these emails is to steal sensitive and valuable data such as bank account details, credit card numbers, login credentials, company financial audits, and much more. To rule them out, you need knowledge in phishing email campaigns and their solutions. You can also consider using email filtering options to block the attacks.

Social Engineering Attacks

It is a new attack used by cyber attackers to gather all the sensitive information about an individual or an organization. It comes in the form of displays of attractive prizes, huge offers, and promotions, advertisements. You will fall prey immediately. You provide your bank account details. All the details you provide ere will be cloned and used for fraudulent financial transactions, identity frauds, crimes, and so on.

Since 2007, the ZEUS virus acted as a social engineering attack used for stealing bank account details and other banking related details from unsuspecting people across the world. They not only come with financial issues but can also lead to downloads of highly destructive threats to your system, which may affect its functioning and capabilities.

The History of Cybersecurity

Cybersecurity is not that old in the technology sector as it dated back to 40 years ago when words like worms, spyware, malware, or viruses meant a different thing. Not only in the information technology sector but for any common man in the business sector, organization, and so on. Since its beginning, it brought mixed reactions as it came as a result of a research project. It is a fantastic fact from the 1970s. Robert Thomas was a researcher for BBN technologies in Cambridge, Massachusetts, at the time he created the computer worm referred to as 'the creeper.' During that time, the creeper infected several computers by attacking one machine after the other with the message; "I'm THE CREEPER: CATCH ME IF YOU CAN."

It was an aggressive threat. Afterward, Ray Tomlinson, the inventor, and creator of email created a similar program referred to as 'the Reaper.' It was to be an antivirus that would delete and clear the creeper.

In the late 1980s, there was another creation of a man called Robert Morris, whose idea was to test the size of the internet. He then wrote a program that would invade the networks, UNIX terminals, and copied itself. The plan referred to was the Morris worm. It was such an aggressive worm that it was disabled and slowed down the functionality of the computer, leaving them unusable. He was the first person to be convicted under the computer fraud and abuse act.

Since then, there has been the creation of invasive, aggressive, and deadliest computer viruses that are prone to cure and are hard to control and detect. That is the main reason that brought about the idea of cybersecurity to help protect data against these deadly attacks.

The Importance of Cybersecurity

Cybersecurity is so critical in an organization or the workplace as the results that felt with its absence are unfriendly. Recently, the increase in threats that led to a lot of damage to individuals and organizations. Handling this cyber menace is hard and needs a lot of effort to ensure all your data is safe and protected from unauthorized persons.

There is a need to ensure you have the right strategies to protect your data from threats and minimizing the damages in the event of attacks. However, to be safer, you need a good grip on the knowledge of cybersecurity fundamentals.

Here are the reasons as to why cybersecurity needs implementation at large:

- There is an aggressive rise in threats and cyber-attacks. For this reason, most organizations are finding it necessary to upgrade their cybersecurity not to fall prey to these attacks. It is a common issue and is taking a toll on individual, organization, banking, business information, which later leads to losses and destruction. It has been witnessed in several countries and giving it the attention it requires will save you a lot. There have been cases where cybercrimes and attacks have cost people up to billions in shillings every year, and that is very alarming.

- There is an increase in techniques and strategies used by the cyber attackers on reaching their targeted persons. They are using more advanced ways to attack, and that has been proven more destructive. They have learned about modern technology and how well to create their malicious threats to affect data to gain profit. That is why you need to learn about cybersecurity and its implementation to keep up with the advancements. It is not that easy mastering all the protective measures, but learning how well to protect your data from the attackers could keep you safe for longer.

- There are new regulations on data protection from GDR, who are expecting every organization to protect the data at their disposal. It is essential due to the increased threats to see to it that your sensitive data is protected and taken care of. In recent times, due to many cases of threats, there are new developments in the courts regarding data theft. To be on the safe side, protecting your information is more important than a long time wasted in the courts.

- Cyber-attacks are very demanding. Once you are affected by threats or attacks, it will take a toll on your resources and organization. There are cases you need to pay ransoms to clear the risks but without surety of getting your information intact. Depending on who took your data, you may end up in reputation breaches and a total financial problem on your business and so on. You can prevent all these scenarios by getting the right preventive measure and ensure your data is protected.

What Are Cybersecurity Fundamentals?

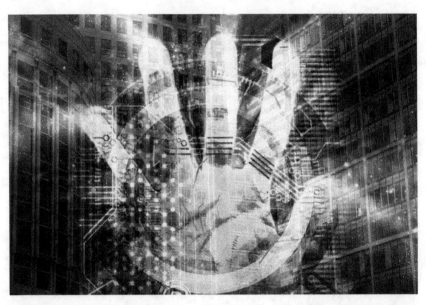

For cybersecurity to be thoroughly analyzed, it follows three basic concepts referred to as 'the CIA Triad,' including confidentiality, integrity, and availability. This model was designed to offer guidance to organizations, institutions, or companies to form an effective security policy. They are essential as their working together will ensure you get the best results in resolving your Cybersecurity issues about information security. These include:

• Confidentiality

This concept is beneficial in limiting the access o any

information. It works ion restricting sensitive and vulnerable information from being accessed by third parties such as hackers and cyber attackers. In any organization, for example, there is a need to protect one's information for easy access as that may cause problems if breached. For this reason, organizations and institutions avoid sharing information and educate their workers or colleagues on the effects and how well to protect the data they hold using secure and robust passwords.

You can easily protect your data by handling it differently. You do not have to make the task too complicated. Making the people in an organization have the idea of how dangerous it is to have your information out there for people to access can significantly help. However, at some point, it may prove a daunting task at first but may greatly be improved by sharing experiences with the affected persons.

To ensure there is confidentiality, you can use data classification, data encryption, biometric verification, and two-factor classification as well as security tokens.

- **Integrity**

Integrity gives you the guarantee of accurate, trustworthy, correct, and consistent data that is unchanged over some time. To protect your data in the transit from third users, ensure it is original, meaning; the data is not changed, altered, deleted, or allowed illegal access. The safety of data starts with you. Letting other people into your information is very risky.

Putting up proper data protection and security measures in your workplace, institution, or organization will guarantee your data of safety. For this to work, there needs to be user access rules and control as well as file permissions to avoid data breaches and sharing. Ensure a trusted system or person handle the data files. Not everybody can process your information the same way; some may have a hidden agenda.

It is a need to monitor your data against theft, threats, and breaches. All this requires an advanced tool and equipment. These tools ensure your information is intact at all times, and if any risk is detected, the organization will know about it and create ways of amending the issue. In most cases, organizations prefer the use of tools such as cryptographic checksum and checksum to verify their data and information integrity.

Moreover, some attacks or threats can lead to data loss or destruction. For this, there is a need for an effective and reliable backup plan. In most cases, cloud backups are the number one trusted solutions as per now.

• Availability

In this case, you need to have your systems in the right condition. Which includes the software, hardware, devices, networks, and security equipment. To give the best results, they should be up to date and well maintained. It will ensure you have proper functionality and easy access to all the data you need without any hindrances. It will also guarantee healthy communication within the system, having a reliable bandwidth.

You will also need to look for types of equipment that are effective for disaster management. In cases of disaster, system attacks, or threats, there needs to be tools and utilities that will help you solve your issues. In this case, disaster recovery plans, firewalls, effective backup plans, and proxy servers are among the best services you can consider as attack solutions.

For these utilities to work accordingly, they should undergo multiple layers of security to determine the safety of constituents of cybersecurity. In most cases, this feature involves networks, computers, hardware systems, or software programs involving the data shared through them.

For an organization to reap results of safe and reliable data storage and protection, there ought to support from both ends. For instance, in an organization, a practical cyber approach, there is a need to involve the people, computers, networks, processes as well as the technology in large or small scale or individually. Realizing a future with fewer cyber-attacks and threats requires a better organization and support systems that work together. You may also be amazed by how

many solutions you can come up with to detect the threats
and solve them.

Chapter 5: What Are the Concepts of Networking?

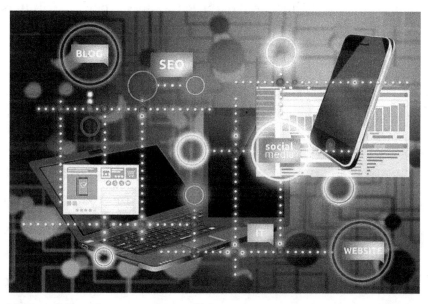

Networking is a series of interconnection of computers worldwide to form an overall structure or system. The base or core for networking includes: types of computer networks, types of network equipment/the hardware, Ethernet, wireless local area network, internet service provider, TCP/IP, and other internet protocols and Net routing, switching and bridging.

There are three critical types of computer networks that are geographically based. These include the Local Area Network (LAN), the Wider Area Network (WAN), and the Metropolitan Area Network (MAN). LAN involves the interconnection of computers within a specific locality covering a small geographical area. It is majorly within buildings. There are further three types of LAN technology, which include Ethernet, Token Ring, and Fiber Distributed Data Interconnect (FDDI). The three categories of LAN are based on a specific arrangement of elements in the computer network. Ethernet LANs is based on a bus topology and broadcast communication. The Token Ring LANs are based on a ring topology. The (FDDI) uses optical fibers and an improved Token Ring mechanism based on two rings flowing in opposite directions. The WANs is an interconnection of computers covering a larger geographical area than the LANs, probably between cities and countries. Here, data is transmitted using such media as fiber optic cable and satellite in most cases. It is based on packet switching technology in which information is transmitted over a digital network is grouped into packets. Examples of WAN technology include Asynchronous Transfer Mode (ATM) and Integrated Services Digital Network (ISDN). Metropolitan Area Network is the interconnection of computers covering a much larger geographical area than WANs. The interconnection here is majorly between continents. The equipment sending data in this case to any significant distance is probably sending it to a minicomputer or a mainframe computer. Data is transmitted using terminal emulation software on the personal computer. This is because more extensive networks are designed to be accessed by terminals. A personal computer emulates or imitates a terminal.

Without networks, we wouldn't accomplish much. Just as human networks make us more efficient, so do computer networks. In business, networks are extremely important. All business operations depend on various forms of networking. Networking helps organizations to save time and money. It also helps organizations and individuals to create new streams of income.

Some concepts shape networking. At first glance, these concepts may seem complex. But if you familiarize yourself with the principles of computer networking, it gets easier.

The reality is that networks are everywhere, and we all work within them. You are used to them to such an extent that you don't even realize it. In this article, we will focus on the concepts of networking. Our main objective is to help you have a better grasp of networking.

A network is a group of several entities that are connected in one way or another. This could be objects or people. It allows the flow of information among the entities involved. However, this has to happen under a set of clear guidelines.

In this piece, we'll be focusing on computer networking. An individual computer can help you accomplish a particular basic task. It undoubtedly boosts your productivity. But when you are using numerous computers that are connected, your productivity becomes greater.

Computers use data networks to process and share important information. Ten staff members can access important information at the same time without sharing a computer. Networking makes it possible for them to do so on different computers. This is made possible by a bunch of interconnected computers. It certainly enhances and promotes coordination within a team working for a common goal.

Imagine what would happen without a network. A team would solely have to rely on one computer to get work done. This could greatly undermine the team's productivity. The team would need a lot of time to complete simple tasks.

Therefore, a computer network can best be described as a group of computers that are linked together. The linking may be done through physical lines. The ultimate goal is to enable efficient exchanging of information in terms of speed and convenience.

When one computer is connected to another, the output is increased. And when several networks are linked together, they form one powerful network. This helps employees to have access to a larger pool of information. With such resources at their disposal, you can rest assured that they can accomplish a lot more.

Components of Network

There are four essential components of a computer network. These are networking devices, end devices, protocols, and the media.

- **End Devices**

Networking takes between devices. End devices play the role of data transmission. They either send or receive various types of data. These are laptops, PCs, phones, or tablets. A network needs at least two devices to function. There are server devices that are tasked with providing data and client devices that depend on the data provided.

- **Media**

Devices have to be connected through a special medium. This medium is known as the media. There are two forms of media. That's the wired and wireless media.

Wireless media uses signals while wired media uses cables.

- **Protocols**

Protocols are important rules in networking. They aid communication between the devices and also set the standards of communication. Normally, protocols can initiate as well as terminate any form of communication between devices. Also, they encrypt the data before it is sent. The data packaged in a form that can be transmitted within the relevant channels.

- **Networking Devices**

84

In between devices, there is a networking device. A networking device's main role is to control the flow data between the end devices. It also forwards the data. This device is categorized into three categories. That's the connecting device, securing device, and forwarding device.

Classification Based on Access Type

The classification based on access types includes Intranet, Extranet, and the Internet.

- **Intranet**

An intranet is a private network. External users can't access this network whatsoever. Not unless they use some unscrupulous methods to do so.

- **Extranet**

An extranet is also a private network. The resources within this network are not available to the public. External are only granted access through a strict authorization process. Full access is not granted to external users. Whatever access they may be given is partial.

- **Internet**

The internet is an open network that anyone with a computer can access. It has a vast resource that the public can utilize.

Classification Based on Relationships between Relevant Devices

This classification is based on the relationship between the end devices. The network is classified into two. That's the peer to peer network and client-server network that will be covered in great detail later.

Networking Plan

When creating a network of computers, you ought to have a network plan. This is because numerous computers are used, hence the need to manage them. Also, you want to ensure that information is kept within particular confines.

The connections should be planned to control the flow of information. Employees should have access to the information that's relevant to their duties. A computer network doesn't mean that everybody in the organization is allowed to access all the information available.

The plan should give clear guidelines on where various types of information should be stored. A plan also defines what information will be accessed by the employees at a given time.

Networking Types and Structures

Networking types are structured differently. They can either be wired or wireless. Also, they could be a combination of both. About a decade ago, most networks were wired. The computer network landscape has since changed. Modern networks mix both wired and wireless connections. Wired networks use Ethernet technology.

Advantages of Wired Networks

- Wired networks are not only reliable but also fast and secure.
- Ethernet ports can also be found in most computing devices, including laptops and desktops.

Disadvantages of Wired Networks

- Wired networks must use cables. And it is costly to run cables.
- Using a wired network within buildings is challenging. This is due to the sophisticated infrastructure. Multiple cables would be required to run between the buildings.
- A wired network doesn't support devices such as smartphones and tablets.

Wireless Networks

Wireless networks don't rely on cables. These networks used the Wi-Fi protocol to transmit data.

Advantages of Wireless Networks

- They are easy to set up. Moreover, you don't require multiple cables running from one point to the other.

- A wireless network offers great flexibility and convenience. They can be used in public places, offices, and homes. Mobile devices use a wireless network. Therefore, you can use all your internet supported devices at your convenience.

Disadvantages of Wireless Networks

- A wireless network is certainly not as secure as a wired network.
- A wireless network is also commonly limited by range. Once you get out of the stipulated range, you can't use it.
- Wireless networks are much slower. The connectivity isn't as fast as it is with a wired network.

Networking Layout and Topologies

To expand a network, the nodes have to be connected. You might not need this in your small office, but as you expand, you'll certainly need it. Though there are many ways to connect these nodes, some of the most common methods include Bluetooth, Wi-Fi, and so on.

These methods of connection are built on various topologies. The common ones are:

- Ring
- Bus
- Mesh

- Hybrid
- Star

Each topology has its strengths and weak points. Wi-Fi and modern Ethernet use a hybrid topology. The hybrid topology is a combination of bus and star. Bluetooth and Wi-Fi can also run on a mesh topology.

Networking Topology – Logical Vs. Physical

The physical connection of network nodes doesn't necessarily dictate how they communicate. Typically, small offices and home networks use the physical bus topology.

- **Peer to Peer Networking**

In peer to peer networking, all the involved nodes are considered to be equal. All nodes can communicate free with each other.

There are no superior nodes with special responsibilities in this kind of networking.

- ○ **Advantages of Peer to Peer Networking**
  - ◆ The peer to peer network doesn't depend on a single node. It is, therefore, unlikely that the failure of a single node will undermine the entire network.

- Additionally, peer to peer network isn't sophisticated. This makes it easy to set up.
- A peer to peer network is quite reliable and resilient. It doesn't breakdown without a good reason.
- This network comes with an excellent distribution of data traffic. And that makes it tremendously effective.
- The hardware used in peer to peer networking is inexpensive. So, the initial cost of running this network is affordable.
- Most networks require a strong central administrator. However, the peer to peer network doesn't rely on a central administrator.

o **Disadvantages**
  - It is challenging to secure a peer to peer network. This makes it susceptible to threats.
  - Every network requires a backup. Nonetheless, peer to peer the network is difficult to back up.
  - Locating information on a peer to peer network isn't easy.

- **Client-Server**

A client-server network is based on a superior server. The

server is tasked with a special role. For example, it could be a control or a web server.

The client has to connect to the server to use certain services. An example of this type of networking is the internet web.

- o **Advantages**

  - ♦ The client-server network is administered with the utmost ease.
  - ♦ It has a specially dedicated node that makes locating of information extremely easy.
  - ♦ A client-server has exceptional safety levels.
  - ♦ This network is easy to manage.

- o **Disadvantages**
  - ♦ Servers can fail. When they fail, the network is jeopardized. These are single points of failure that greatly undermine the entire network.
  - ♦ The client-server hardware doesn't come cheap. It requires a significant investment, which can be out of rich for both homes and small office owners.
  - ♦ This network can get concentrated at some point. This may cause some downtime within a network.

♦ The best modern examples of a client-server network include Twitter, Facebook, and Google Search.

Classification of Computer Networks

Computer networks are classified into various categories. The classifications are based on geographical locations, the relationship between the devices used, and access types.

Classification Based on Geographical locations

LAN-Local Area Network: It links devices within one office or several offices. Ethernet and Token Ring fall within this category.

MAN-Metropolitan Area Network: It is a slightly larger network with the capacity to connect devices across buildings.

WAN-Wide Area Network: This is a massive network that links devices to multiple devices across countries. A good example of the WAN network includes the Asynchronous Transfer Mode and the Integrated Services Digital Network.

PAN-Personal Area Network: This network is used within a personal area to link devices. It is the kind of network that you use to link your laptop to a printer.

Networking Layers and Protocols

A protocol is a predetermined set of guidelines that dictates how computers should communicate with each other. HTTP is one of the popular protocols, which you may have across in your interactions with computers. This protocol supports communication between a particular web browser and its server.

Good examples of data link protocols include are Wi-Fi and Ethernet. These protocols shape the data as it appears on the media. Both of them use a physical address that's referred to as the MAC address. It has a capacity of 48 bits.

Other popular MAC addresses include the EUI 64 that has 64 bits.

Networking can be divided into numerous layers or levels.

There is the OSI network that utilizes a seven-layer model. Also, there is a common TCP/IP network, which uses a four-layer model. Here are the four levels of the TCP/IP network, and their respective examples:

- Data link-level- Ethernet or Wi-Fi.
- Transport level- UDP or TCP.
- Networking-IP
- Application level-HTTP

As the sending process is progress, these layers add a distinct header to the data. The headers are then systematically eliminated as the data moves towards its destination.

Transmission Control Protocol

TCP provides a safe mode of transmitting data. The transmission takes place through IP packets. The packets have accurate error detection capability. All the data that's transmitted in packets reach as their destination as sent. Data can't be accidentally altered in any way. You can rest assured that the data reaches its destination in its original order.

Before the process of transmitting data is initiated, there has to be a safe connection between the computers involved.

- It is the role of TCP to convert the data into packets.
- Other Applications Protocol in Networking
- FTP (File Transfer Protocol)
- File transfer protocol aids the transfer of various files of data between two computers. The computers need to have an active internet connection.
- Telnet (Terminal Protocol)
- Sometimes, the user needs to connect to a terminal mode. The terminal protocol enables the user to do so.
- SMTP (Simple Mail Transfer Protocol)
- SMTP is a protocol that simply the electronic mail service.

Chapter 6: Information Tech Guide

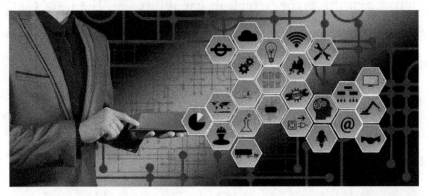

Computer technology is used to assist and link people in the contemporary world in many ways. The laptops, desktops, and mobile phones they all network together to perform multiple operations at the same time. The government, individual, and organization depend on these devices for essential things like in the entertainment, food production, communication, education, care, and transportation.

Understanding Information Technology

Information technology – It is the use of a computer, network, storage, and other devices into to secure process, create, store electronic data or information, and exchange all manner of electronic data. Computer technology is the study of computer networks and developing several software programs. It comprises of computer database design, programming, and networking. All these programs correlate to ensure that a computer works properly.

A computer machine is a programmable device that is designed to operate arithmetic and logical operation given by the user and provides a desirable processed output. The computer has two major categories, which are hardware and software. The hardware consists of all layers of physical and tangible components of a computer, such as CPU (central processing unit), keyboard, monitor mouse, and motherboard. While Software is the instructions stored in a computer to run the hardware, these instructions command the computer to perform a specific task, and such Software is operating systems and applications.

Computer technology is any machine that takes commands and calculates the instructions accordingly; the operation can be record-keeping, bailing, planning, and transactions. All these operations take place in a commercially available machine that has been customized according to their functionality. Such machines that are common to our daily process are gas station pumps, ATM, barcode scanners, and GPS units. However, each of those machines they all rely on circuit boards and digital data to meet the demand and needs of the customer.

Most customers gain improvement in access to services

through the internet by ordering products, send emails, scan the barcode through a smartphone, and read reviews before purchasing anything on the website. Most of the programs in television use audio, visual, and animation and special effects in the production of their programs. Audiovisual games employ graphics created by a computer and plugged in a laptop or home-based entertainment where the player can play by themselves or with others using the internet.

The use of applications on the mobile phone can be beneficial in the following ways:

make order in a restaurant, preservation in a hotel, book an appointment with a doctor, purchase movie tickets usually save time that could have been used to wait in a queue.

Hardware

Computer hardware are physical, tangible components of a computer they include. Examples are:

Monitor, control unit (CU), keyboard, mouse, motherboard, central processing unit (CPU), hard driver, random access memory (RAM), and power supply.

1. CPU

It is considered to be the mind of the computer machine that performs all kinds of operations like data processing, storage of data, and instructions. CPU controls all the activities that make up a computer. There are three components of a CPU:

- **ALU (Arithmetic Logic Unit)**

It is the logical part of the CPU in a computer. When you need to carry out mathematical or logical decisions in a computer, the information is carried out by ALU. The ALU contemplates the information in bits. Bits are binary logic 0's and 1" s. They are made up of memories built in the CPU know as registers, which are used to hold data, and data at this point is classified as binary information. They are processed accordingly to instructions.

- **CU (Control Unit)**

It is a component of a CPU in a computer that guides the operation of the processor. It communicates to the computer memory, output, and input devices and ALU on how to respond to the database instruction and does not process any data.

- **Memory**

Memory is a part of a computer that stores data and information that is necessary for functioning. There are two types of memories:

- Ram – Random Access Memory is the internal memory of the CPU that is responsible for storing data, programs, and the result of an application. The mind is read and writes hence volatile meaning stores data when the computer is working. When the machine is switched off, data is lost or erased. Examples of RAM are Dynamic Random Access Memory (DRAM) - it is a physical memory used in personal computers. This type of memory must be continuously refreshed, or it loses its contents, and it is economical. Static Random Access Memory (SRAM) – this memory is faster and less volatile than DRAM; hence requires more power and very expensive and does not require to be refreshed. Synchronous Dynamic Random Access Memory this memory has a higher processing speed.

- **Read-Only Memory (ROM)** – this type of memory where you can only read, but you cannot write. This kind of memory is non-volatile. The information stored in this memory in permanent, the memory stores instructions that are required to start a computer machine or bootstrap. They are many types of ROM. Examples are MROM (Masked ROM), Programmable Read-only

Memory, Erasable and Programmable Read-Only Memory and EPROM

2. Peripherals

These are devices connected to the computer externally when these devices are disconnected to the computer will still function, but the functions performed by the peripheral will not be available. Examples of peripheral are;

- **Monitor**

A monitor is a visual display unit and is the primary output device of a computer. They display images as small dots called pixels that are arranged in a computer in a rectangular form that sharpens the images. The size of an image will depend on the number of pixels used.

- **Keyboard**

It is an input device that helps to input data into a computer. It consists of keys that are responsible for inputting alphabets, numbers, and special characters into a computer. They can also navigate using the keyboard to perform a particular shortcut in a computer machine.

- **Mouse**

It is a pointing device that uses cursor. A control device that has a small box with a corpulent ball at its base, which intellects the movement of the mouse and sends the signals to the CPU to process data.

- **Printer**

It is an output device that is used to print processes data into a paper. Examples of printers are: Impact printers- They write the data by striking the ribbon, which is usually pressed on the document to print. Non-impact printers – this kind of printers print the characters without using the ribbon. They print the whole page of a paper at a time. They are a laser printer, page printer, or inkjet printers.

- **Joy Stick**

This kind of peripherals moves the cursor into a position in a monitor and used in a Computer-Aided Design (CAD).

- **Scanner**

This device allows the user to san printed papers and converts them into a file that is used in a computer device.

Wireless and LTE

These are devices that change electrical signals into waves; they connect a wired network using Wi-Fi. They are three main types of wireless devices which are WAN, PAN, and LAN. Wireless Wide Area Network made through the use of mobile phone signals. They are created and maintained by a mobile phone service provider. Wireless local area network uses radio waves, but the backbone of these networks are sustained using cables with a wireless access point connecting the network. This kind of wireless can be used in a room to being used in an entire university or a hospital. Wireless Personal Area Network (WPAN) they are a form of network that is short in range. They use Bluetooth technology and commonly interconnect compatible devices near the central location. The range of WPAN has a variety of thirty feet.

The devices that are used by networks vary from computers, tablets, phones, and laptops and refer to as clients. When accessing the network through hotspot or use of a router in office or home, the device is referred to as the client. Some router can operate as a client; this can happen when a card is in a computer and connect to other access points or connect to more detached Apps. The Apps can be a standalone device that bridges between a wireless and an Ethernet or a router. The Apps can cover a wide range of areas using wireless networks depending on the power of the computer and type of antenna used by the device.

Some phones, laptops, or wireless router, can support a mode known as Ad-Hoc that allows the device to connect directly together without an access point between that controls the connections. Not all the computers have the Ad-Hoc, and some are hidden. The devices that Ad-Hoc enabled to create a mesh of network, and when they are enabled is called Mesh Nodes.

The wireless network that connects distance areas like two building they need a more focused antenna such as dish antenna. Dish antenna sent thin beams of the network into a specific direction. This long-distance coverage is called point to point connection; this means that two points are connected. The process requires two devices, one configured to the Access point and the other one as a client.

LTE (Long Term Evolution)

It is a term mostly used as 4G LTE and is the standard wireless data. The transmissions that allow one to watch their favorite documentary online or download and watch it later very fast.4g wireless communication was developed by the 3rd generation partnership project that provides ten times the speed of the 3G network on a mobile phone.

The 4G technologies are designed to provide an IP address based on data, voice, and multimedia streaming.

An Overview of LTE

This is a name given to 3GPP evolved, standard requirement to deal with the increasing data throughout the provision of market. The group that started to work with 3GPPRANstanderdized for LTE in late 2004, and by 20017, all the LTE features that ware related to its functionality ware finished. And in early 2018, most performances specification and protocol ware finished and released.

LTE Requirements

Requirements are written, and defined concept from scuff, absolute fashion, and others meant relation to UTRA nomenclature. The following are LTE design parameters:

- Mobility of up to 350km/h
- Spectrum flexibility, seamless coexistence with other previous technologies hence reduced flexibility and cost
- All systems should support data rates of 100 Mbps in a downlinked 50mbps in the uplink, within a 20MHz bandwidth or a spectral efficiency value of 5bps/Hz and 2.4bps/Hz respectively.
- Downlink and uplink use throughput per MHz at five %point of CDF

The 4g is ten times faster than 3G, can download something at a speed of 22 and 5 Mbps, while 4G is a significant improvement over 3G. Most cellular phones caries and advertise their network as 4G LTE, as it sounds the same as 4G, and some of the cell phones display a 4G LTE. 4G and 4G

106

LTE differences;

The consumer can tell the difference between a 4G and LTE by the speed of downloading something. The mobile phone companies are always updating their cellular LTE network and are closing a gap between a 4G and LTE. The LTE-A is the currently fastest option available right now.

Standard Definitions on Wireless and LTE

Antenna – Converts the electrical signals into radio waves and generally connected to a radio device that transmits the messages into a radio receiver and the interface between the electrical signals in radio and the movement of indicators through the inflight.

Ad-Hoc Network – this is a Device network that is available in a laptop or computer machine connections and is shown as a computer to computer networks. The Ad-hoc can be unplanned or decentralizes network connections.

AP (Access Point) – these are devices that allow other wireless devices to connect into a wired network using Wi-Fi.

Ethernet – This is a type of networking protocol that defines some cable and connections that are used for wiring devices together. In most cases, the Ethernet cabling is categorized into five or six e.g., a cell phone, computer, or tablet.

Node – this is an individual device in a mesh net of the network.

Power over the internet – these describe as the system which passes electrical control along with figures on Ethernet cabling.

Cabling

A cable network is a service delivery that supplies the devices like computer, television or a laptop programs that a user has subscribed to. The availability of such depends on the local franchise area. The number of available channels and networks will depend on some factors. The average cable viewer has the option of viewing more than 150 networks through a cable subscription. The cable system manager decides on the channels and networks to be carried on a specific place. The channel and network are selections are based on the viewer analysis and franchise agreement with the viewer.

Types of Cable Network

They are three different types of a cable network:
Basic, pay and pay per view. The basic network is available per at the lowest and is very popular for people whose budget is limited. There are at least 60 cable channels that can be defined as a first cable network.

The pay cable network is those that charge a flat monthly subscription. The flat-rate payment is required as the network does not run any television advertisement. Hence they need some monthly subscription in order to profit the company. A movie TV station is a good example of such a network.

Pay per view cable network is TV channels that charge a fee for every individual program watched. The pay-per-view program is a network that shows movies that can be rented and viewed. Other programs allow the customer to go and watch the program elsewhere, like the movie theatre.

Choosing a Cable Network

You can only choose one cable network; each cable provider tends to offer cable packages that deliver different Laval of programs. An example, a basic cable network may provide 60 channels, and premium offers over 100 applications. It's only you who can choose the best package that fits your budget.

Advantages of Cabling Network

It is essential to evaluate the cable network before installation. A net that will make use of physical cabling will be more robust and secure compared to wireless network technology.

Security – This is the most important advantage as the cabling network offers a higher level of security than the wireless networks. However, the measure of protection will include the protected WI-FI network and passwords that help to improve the safety of a wireless network. Hence they can never be securing than the cable network.

Speed – not all the cable networks will provide speedy connections, but the newer types of twisted data cabling can operate up to 10 gigabits. An example is a fiber optic cabling transmits light rather than standard data information, making it optimal for high speed and ranges.

Reduced interference – with a proper installation cabling network will help reduce the interference caused by electrical hitch, known as electrical, mechanical obstruction, and radiofrequency. On the other hand, the wireless network is more susceptible to radio frequency interference.

Consistence connections – Compared to the wireless connection, the cabling is more consistence in connection. When the data is transferred in wireless connections, there is a lapse in network connections caused by electrical interferences.

Expandability – Each router or a hub will provide support of up to 255devices.

Cybersecurity

Cybersecurity is a process or practice that is designed to protect network programs, devices, and data from being attached, authorized access or damaged.

Significance of Cybersecurity

Most of the co-operations and organization collect and stored in a large amount of data in storage devices, a large amount of the data can contain a large amount of sensitive information. Organization and governmental bodies transmit a large amount of raw data across some network and other devices while doing their business. Cybersecurity is dedicated to protecting the information, the programmers, and the system used to store data. The spying on these data are national insecurity and can lead to terrorism.

For an organization to function and coordinate effectively,

they need effective cybersecurity. There are a few elements of excellent cybersecurity. They are:

- Great data security
- Application security
- Network security cloud security
- Endpoint security
- Mobile security
- Disaster recovery continuity plan
- And end-user education on security

The organization is advised to promote proactive measures and adapt more approaches to cybersecurity. The NIST (National Institute of Standards and Technology) issued necessary guidelines on the risk and a framework that recommends a shift on continuous monitoring and data focus approach to cabbing cybersecurity.

How to Managing Cyber Security

The NCSA (National Cyber Security Alliance) gives a recommendation on a top-down approach to cybersecurity, which organization management leads and prioritizing the management of cybersecurity. The NCSA advises all the organizations to be ready and prepared for any eventuality. Cyber risk assessment should be put in place in case of any behavior that impacts the functioning of the organization. The organization should have an outline of the damages that an organization would incur in the case of cyber-attack. The cyber risk assessment should consider any regulation that impacts the way the organization collects, stores, and secures data.

Having the best cybersecurity or combining cybersecurity measures and educating the employees on cyber-attacks is the best effort an organization can do to cab the cyber-attack. It may appear like a difficult task but it always to start small and focus on securing the most sensitive information hence going forward to protecting all the data

In conclusion, information technology helps organizations, individual businesses, and governments to increase their efficiency and improvements in effectively processing information. It helps the consumer to buy and sell new relevant technology devices, thus creating a world of business-minded people. Also, technology creates a safe environment by purchasing and installing CCTV cameras. Regardless, there is a continuity of demand for innovative technology solutions leaving room for advancement.

Network Address

Networks come with an IP address. All devices attached to a network have an IP address. You can locate the device using its IP address.

An IP address (Internet Protocol Address) is assigned to every device in a numerical representation. This is for every device that participates in a computing activity. The device has to be, however, dependent on an internet protocol.

The IPv6 and the IPv4 are the two common versions of the Internet Protocol.

IPv4 has been used since the birth of the internet. It is used both in corporate networks as well as the internet. Networking experts predict that it will be replaced by IPv6 in the future. This is attributed to the fact that the IPv6 has a larger capacity. While the IPv4 is just 32 bits, IPv6 is 128 bits. This means that it can effortlessly accommodate a larger number of devices.

Functions of the IP protocol

During the sending of data, the initial data is decomposed into datagrams. Each datagram has a header. The header consists of the port number of the destination and the IP address.

Datagrams are sent to specific getaways. The process is successive as the getaways are sent from one getaway to the other. This process goes on until the datagrams reach the intended getaways.

Private and Public IP Addresses

You might have heard of private IP addresses. Such addresses are not routable. They can be used in both business and home networks.

On the other hand, public IP addresses are routable. They travel on the internet.

Assigning of IP Addresses

In case you are wondering how IP addresses are assigned, we will tell you how.

For modern networks, IP addresses are assigned automatically. This happens under the DHCP. It doesn't mean that they can't be assigned manually. It is possible, but only on rare occasions.

Domain Names and IP Addresses

People prefer to use names as a form of address. Names are easy to remember. But computers use numbers. If you type a domain name into a web browser, the system translates into an IP address. A DNS server that's found on the internet is tasked with the translation process.

Data Transmission

There is a lot of data transmission that takes place within a network. How does it take place? Data transmission is done through packet switching. The messages are first segmented into segments that are known as packets. The packets are then transmitted from one computer to the next. Upon delivery, data is then extracted from each of these packets. The original message is then reconstructed.

The packets are well-coiffed. They have a data area and a header. Headers consist of two addresses. That's the source and the destination address. Additionally, the header carries sequencing information that helps to reconstruct the original message.

Importance of Networks

A computer machine has been designed for the sole purpose of manipulating data. When computers are linked together, great things are accomplished. The networks are instrumental in the sharing of information and other resources among people. These resources include the internet, file sharing, and applications.

Networks make it easy for colleagues to communicate either through email or other platforms available on the internet. The same applies to industrial computers because the information has to be shared constantly.

Networking enables businesses to save money. For example, instead of buying a printer for all your employees, you can use networking to link one printer to many computers. This allows all your employees to share a single printer effectively. Similarities between Different Types of Networks

Although there are various types of networks, there is a

similarity between them. For example, networks share servers. These are computers that are endowed with sharable resources within a particular network.

Other Similarities

The server serves clients. Clients are computers that access depends on the information held on the server. They all access the pool of information offered by a network server.

A Connection medium that enhances the connection of several computers within a network

Another similarity is computer peripherals. Printers and files are also used within different networks.

As you can see, computer networking is a well-structured process that makes work easy. Government agencies and business organizations use to rely on networking to streamline their functions. Networking saves such organizations millions of dollars every year.

Besides that, networking helps organizations to work more efficiently. Teams can tackle various projects with much ease when they network.

Networking aids the sharing of important information between the involved parties. Organizations store massive information. It is difficult to store, manage, and process the data manually. Moreover, organizations are large. And all the data that's gathered and used can be overwhelming.

Apart from the complex duties that simplified by networking, there are other minor but equally important functions. For example, networking aids the configuration of various computers in an office. This enables the employs to share the fax machine, or a printer through a network.

It is not only a large organization that benefits from networking. In this digital area, all types of businesses depend on networks. Therefore, it is important to be familiar with the concepts of networking.

Chapter 7: What Are the Best Network Monitoring Tools?

Networking is also referred to as computer networking. It is a term used to refer to transportation and exchange of data between nodes through a universal medium in the information system. Networking involves using a network, designing construction, managing, maintaining, and operating the network software, infrastructure, and policies. Networking allows for the connection of devices and endpoints together on a local area network or a bigger network. This is one of the most effective services that business owners all over the world can take advantage of. Computer networking provides valid and reliable ways of resources and information sharing within an organization or a business. It helps people to benefit from their information technology equipment and systems.

The significant benefits of networking include:

File sharing – Data can be easily shared among different users. Data can as well be accessed remotely when it is kept on other connected devices.

Resource sharing – Computer networking helps in sharing resources between different peripheral devices connected to the network. They include copiers, scanners, and printers. Resource sharing helps to save money because the software can as well be shared among different users.

Sharing one Internet connection – Having a single internet connection is cost-efficient and enhances the protection of systems when the network is adequately secured.

Increasing the storage capacity – Networking allows for the access of multimedia, and vital files when they are stored remotely in other networks- connected storage devices and machines.

Computer networking also improves communication in that customers, staff, and suppliers easily share information and keep in touch. It allows for everyone interested in business access common databases, thus avoiding duplication of data,

121

preventing errors, and saving time. Networking also makes it easier for organizational staff to work on queries, thus delivering better standards of service. The improvements are possible because of customer's data sharing through the networks.

Computer networking also has incredible benefits on costs. Information is stored in one standard and centralized database, thus increasing the efficiency of the drive and reducing costs. Staffs are able to deal with many customers in little time because they are all accessing product and customer databases. Minimum IT support is also required because network administration can be efficiently centralized. Sharing of internet access, and peripherals sharing cam also help in cutting costs.

Improving consistency and reducing errors are other significant benefits of computer networking. This is because all staff in a business or organization are accessing similar information and from a single source. It allows for the easier making of standard version manuals and directories accessible to each staff. Backing up of data from individual points on a scheduled basis provides for consistency.

The skills required when operating computer networking entirely depends on the network's complexity. Large enterprises, for instance, may have more security requirements due to multiple nodes. Such companies, therefore, require experienced network administrators who can successfully manage and maintain the network. This may be different from smaller organizations whereby there are few nodes involved, thus requiring less security.

Basic Fundamentals of Computer Networking

Computer networking has been in existence for quite a long time, and as years go by, advancements continue to be made. Networking involves multiple devices such as routers, computers, and switches being connected to each other through wireless signals or cables. Building a wireless network needs one to understand all the basics of joining networks.

Many people have an aim of becoming expert IT technicians, and understanding only the hardware may not be so helpful to them. Many people get stuck at the networking point due to misunderstandings. The paragraphs below will explain some of the basic fundamentals of networking. They will give an understanding of how computers communicate through networks. Understanding the interaction and communication between computers is essential to anyone who wants to become a networking administrator.

Networking protocols are essential for developers dealing with applications relating to servers that use JAVA or programming based on Socket, such as bash or python, as well as System Admin. Computer networking is done through diverse sets of IP protocol suites. The most popularly used protocols include IP and TCP. IP is an abbreviation for Internet Protocols. Each of the protocols has unique architecture, as well as diverse functionalities.

The Internet Protocol

The internet protocol gives the definition of the networking communication protocols principals. It is helpful in relaying many datagrams through network boundaries. The internet protocol's primary purpose is providing routing functions that help in the establishment of inter-networking connection, enabling the internet. The primary function is delivering packets from one host to the other host while depending on present IP addresses. The IP addresses are available on the packets' headers.

The internet protocols have four layers, with each layer having a set of instructions it carries out. The four layers include the application layer, the data link layer, the network layer, and the transport layer.

1. The Basic Fundamental of Networking Layer – The Application Layer

The application layer appears at the topmost of IP and TCP protocols in networking. The primary purpose of the layer is transferring data through computers from a particular end to the other. The application layer works in conjunction with processes and applications using transport layer protocols. The processes and applications transport explicit instructions that help in the execution of tasks and enhances communication with the second layer. Application layer protocols have the following elements.

Hypertext transfer protocol that is commonly applied in modern webs. It provided a base for the founding of the World Wide Web. The protocol acts in the form of requesting and responding. It engages in multiple activities for the client.

File transfer protocol engages in the transfer of data to several networks. Its main tasks involve transferring and controlling data between computers using client and server architecture models. In many cases, the protocol can either use a password for authentication or can anonymously and automatically connect.

A **simple mail transfer** protocol is used when transmitting emails. The protocol is based on texts. It consists of three elements the MAIL that determines the returning address, RCTP allowing for connection with the recipient, and DATA acting as the message's body.

The simple network management protocol is based on IP addresses. Its principal function is consistently collecting information on IP addresses from different machines. There are many devices that support the use of a simple network management protocol. There are also many diverse versions of the particular protocol.

2. The Basic Fundamental of Networking – The Presentation Layer

The presentation layer works on the translation or converting data, for instance, encoding character, and compressing data between software applications, and networking devices. It is considered to be efficient when dealing with secure transactions such as money transfer and banking. It is useful because it allows for encryption and decryption of such reliable data. The presentation layer also helps in the conversion of formats.

3. The Networking Session Layer

As a basic fundamental in networking, the networking session layer has the responsibility of opening, closing, and managing end-user application's sessions. The sessions can include many requests and responses taking place inside the software. The layer also facilitates the combinations of packets as well as sorting them in an appropriate order.

4. The Transport Layer

The task of the transport layer is communicating with the application layer about transferring data to the necessary hosts. In performing its role, the transport layer uses the transmission control protocol in most cases due to its reliability. The control protocol helps in the transmission of data from the application layer into smaller sizes of data and later transferring them one by one to the network. It is commonly used when people want to download and upload large files. It ensures there is no loss of packets that could lead to the corruption of downloaded and uploaded data.

5. The Networking Network Layer

The networking network layer is also referred to as the internet layer. Its main purpose is to route data above networks. The Internet protocol is used when differentiating addresses. The internet control message protocol is commonly used in commanding the ping to check on whether the host is active. It also sends error messages through the network, describing if a host is not responding or is down.

6. The Networking Data Link Layer

It is also referred to as the Network Interface Layer. Its main function is providing drivers for diverse devices found in the Operating System. The drivers communicate and transfer data to networks. The network interface card facilitates communication between devices. The transfer of data is done either through cables or wirelessly through routers and Wi-Fi. The significant protocols used in transferring data are the address resolution protocols and point to point protocols.

7. The Networking Physical Layer

The physical networking layer is a vital layer found in the OSI computer networking model. It comprises of networking hardware. It is considered to be the most complex layer in networking due to the diversity of networking devices that are available. Its primary function is transferring raw bits over physical hardware through nodes used for the connection. It comprises of the hardware, including the wireless hardware consisting of Wi-Fi, connectors, cables, and network interface cards.

Understanding Cyber Security

Cybersecurity is also referred to as computer security or information technology security. It is the act of protecting computer systems from damage or theft to their software, hardware, and electronic data. It also means preventing the misdirection and disruption of computer systems from the services they are responsible for providing.

The increase in dependence on computer systems, wireless networks, and the internet has led to the popularity in the field of cybersecurity. It is one of the most concerned matters in the contemporary world due to overgrowing cases of cyber-attacks and threats. Due to its complexity, cybersecurity has also become one of the challenges facing the technology field today.

Cyber attackers are making use of more refined techniques to target and attack computer systems. Small and large organizations, as well as individuals, are being impacted by these cyber threats and attacks. They have considered cybersecurity as a priority in their everyday operations. The focus is on coming up with the best measures to control and eliminate cyber threats and attacks. Employees in organizations are being trained on the best measures to deal with cyber-attacks. Almost everything we do today is linked to the internet, thus increasing chances for vulnerabilities, flaws, and breaches.

Cybersecurity is defined as a process and techniques that are involved in the protection of sensitive data, networks, computer systems, and software applications from potential cyber-attacks. Cyber-attack is a terminology used in covering multiple topics. Most of the common issues covered by cyber-attacks include exploitation of resources, disruption of the normal functioning of businesses and processes involved, tampering systems, and the data stored in them, unauthorized access to sensitive information and targeted systems, and use of ransomware attacks in encryption of data and extortion of money from victims.

Cyber-attacks have been quite innovative, and attackers can disrupt security and hack computer systems. Businesses, therefore, have to come up with strategies through which they can effectively fight back the dangerous attacks. Understanding the importance of cybersecurity needs one to recognize some common forms of attacks and threats.

Ransomware – This is a software program involved in file encryption. It uses exceptional algorithms in robust encryption in encrypting files within the targeted system. Ransomware threat authors, applies a rare key for each target, saving each on a remote server. Users are, therefore, unable to access these files through any application. The attackers take advantage of the situation by extorting money from the victims for decryption of data or providing the decryption code.

Botnets Attacks – The main reason for designing botnets was for them to perform particular tasks in a group. Cyber attackers are, however, using them for all the wrong purposes. They use it by accessing and injecting malware or malicious code that disrupts the functionality of the network. Common botnets include spreading spam emails, stealing of personal data, and distributed denial of service. Large-scale organizations and businesses are primary victims of botnets attacks because of colossal data access.

Social engineering attacks – Cybercriminals are using social engineering attacks strategy to gain computer user's sensitive details. The tactic involves tricking users through attractive prizes, advertisements, huge offers, and requesting the user to feed their confidential and bank account information. The information that users feed is cloned and used in identity and financial fraud.

Cryptocurrency Hijacking – Cryptocurrency hijacking is a new addition in the modern cyber world. Advancement in digital mining and currency has led to an increase of cyber-crimes. Cybercriminals are coming up with ways through which they can benefit from cryptocurrency. Traders and investors who focus on cryptocurrency are becoming primary soft targets for this form of attack. The hijacking process involves designing and injecting mining codes silently to the computer systems. The crypto jacker uses power resources, GPU, and CPU of the target system in mining for cryptocurrency. Monero coins are particularly mined utilizing this kind of technique. The target victim usually incurs the vast internet and electricity bills. The lifespan of the victim devices is also reduced.

Phishing – This is a common cyber-attack whereby the attacker sends a spam email and attempts to imitate any legitimate source. Emails sent through phishing usually have strong messages and are followed by attachments such as big job offers, and an invoice. The aim of the attacker is to steal confidential and sensitive data. They are able to gather information such as credit card numbers, login credentials, and information on bank accounts. Email filtering techniques can help one in avoiding such attacks.

Experiencing cyber-attacks has become so prevalent in most organizations and businesses today. It is vital to research techniques being applied and the measures to avoid these attacks. Educating oneself on the basics of cybersecurity and its use can as well reduce the risks of being attacked.

Cybersecurity is a broad term based on three major concepts. The concepts are named "The CIA Triad." This means that it is comprised of confidentiality, integrity, and availability. The model was designed to act as a guide to businesses and organizations on crucial policies involved in cybersecurity in information technology.

1. Confidentiality

These are the rules that provide some limitations to accessing information. Confidentiality consists in taking appropriate measures to eliminate the risks of confidential and sensitive information being accessed by cyber hackers and attackers. In most organizations and large-scale businesses, people are either denied or allowed access to information depending on how it is categorized. The right person in each department is authorized to access the information. Proper training is also given to these people about using strong passwords to secure their accounts and sharing information. Data protection is enhanced by changing how data is handled.

2. Integrity

Integrity guarantees accuracy, trustworthiness, and consistency of data over a period. It ensures that the data in transit is not altered, deleted, changed, or illegally accessed. Appropriate measures are taken to ensure the safety of the data. A data breach is controlled through user access and file permission control measures. Change or breach in particular data can be detected by the use of appropriate technologies and tools. Regular backups help in coping with potential data loss, unintended deletion, or cyber-attacks.

3. Availability

Availability means that all essential components, such as devices, networks, software, hardware, and security tools, should be adequately maintained and consistently upgraded. This helps in ensuring the proper functioning and data access without disruption. It also means providing consistent communication between multiple components by giving adequate bandwidth. Availability also means providing diverse equipment for security in case of any cyber-attacks. Disaster recovery plans, reasonable backup solutions, firewalls, and proxy servers are efficient utilities in coping with cyber-attacks.

Chapter 8: Types of Firewall

A firewall is a kind of cybersecurity tool that protects a computer network from being tempered or compromised: preventing attacks from hackers who try breaking into the system from outside. Firewalls can be in various forms; it can be in the form of a software or hardware on a computer. For a firewall to work efficiently, it has to be connected to at least two network interfaces with one protected and the other that is exposed to attacks or threats. Therefore, you can consider a firewall to a form of gateway installed between two sets of a network.

How Do Firewalls Work?

Having known what firewalls are and what they do, it is time you learned how they work! Firewalls work by examining all the available data packets that pass through them to assess whether they meet the guidelines and regulations posed by the Access Control List (ACL) and created by the person administrating the network. If the data packets meet the rules set by ACL, they will be allowed to maneuver inside the connection.

Additionally, firewalls play a critical role in keeping a log of essential procedures and activities occurring within a network. Again, the necessary actions are only identified by the administrator. He then configures the related firewall to keep the logs basing on the level of importance.

The process of filtering logs can be done basing on several things, including the packet attributes, address, state, and protocols. Firewalls, however, only display the packet headers on screens.

Having known how firewalls work, we next discuss the types of firewalls. Read on to find out!

The Types of Firewalls

Firewalls are categorized into different types. This is done depending on the level of security they provide and the advancement they have. Below, we discuss extensively on the types of firewalls in existence today.

- **The Packet Filtering Firewall**

This is a type of firewall that is usually installed on routers that connect or link the network in the inside to the internet. The package filtering firewall is only implemented on the OSI model of a network layer. It works based on the rules defined by the Access Control Lists. Packet filtering firewalls work by checking the whole set of packets provided and verify them against the set of instructions provided by the administrator through the ACL. In situations where a package doesn't meet the set of rules defined by the administrator, that packet gets dropped immediately, and logs are informed and update accordingly. When using packet filtering firewalls, administrators have the power to build their ACL basing on the protocol, address, and packet attributes.

- **Advantages of Packet Filtering Firewalls**

    - One of the significant benefits of packet filtering firewalls is that they are very affordable.
    - Packet filtering firewalls also need lower resource usage to make them cost-efficient.
    - Additionally, they are the best suited for those of us with smaller networks.

- **Disadvantages of Packet Filtering Firewalls**

♦ As we mentioned earlier, the packet filtering firewalls only work network layers, and they cannot work on complex instruction based type of models.

♦ Additionally, packet filtering firewalls are also very vulnerable, especially to spoofing on most occasions.

• **The Circuit Level Gateway Firewalls**

This is a type of firewall that is installed at session layers of any OSI model. They are used to monitor events and sessions such as the TCP multiple way handshakes to determine whether the connection requested is legit or not. In circuit-level gateway firewalls, the significant and vital screening takes place before the link is launched. The information channeled to a computer device on the other side of the network via circuit-level gateway looks to have come from a portal. This feature plays a vital role in establishing cover stealth for private networks from strangers.

o **Advantages of Circuit Level Gateway Firewalls**

- Just like the Packet Filtering Firewalls, the circuit-level gateway firewalls are also very affordable and cost-friendly.
- Circuit Level Gateway Firewalls also give the private network anonymity, making it very secure from threats and hackers.

○ **Disadvantages of Circuit Level Gateway Firewalls**

- One of the significant drawbacks of the circuit-level gateway firewalls is they are not able to filter the individual packets. This makes them very vulnerable because once a connection is established, hackers can take advantage of it.

The Application of This Kind of Firewalls

The gateway firewall circuit levels are applied in many dimensions of technology in today's world. The application-level gateways, for instance, are used in the layer one in the application of an OSI tool and can give security and protecting the specific Application Layer of the Protocol in question. One good example of the level application Gateway Firewalls is the proxy server. This kind of firewall, however, can only work with protocols that are highlighted. A good example is, if you installed a web application basing on a firewall, it only will be able to enable the HTTP Protocols Data. The Circuit level gateway firewalls are meant to understand app-specific commands like the HTTP: POST and HTTP: GET as installed on application layers for Special Protocols.

Additionally, the application level firewalls can also be used as the caching servers that play an essential role in improving network performance, making it easier to log the level of traffic.

The Stateful Multilayer Firewall

This firewall is made of a combination of all the firewalls we have discussed so far. They are very advanced firewalls and complex in equal measure. Stateful Multilayer Inspection Firewalls can be used to filter the packets in network layers through the use of ACLs.

Additionally, the Stateful Multilayer Inspection firewall also checks for the single sessions provided on the session layers as well as evaluating packets on the ALG. This type of firewall is compatible with transparent mode enabling direct linkage and connections between the server and the client, something that wasn't possible a few years ago. The Stateful multilayer inspection firewall implements the algorithms and critical security models that are specified by protocols; hence, in the long run, making data transfer and connections easier and secure.

The Proxy Firewalls

These kinds of firewalls operate in application layers with the primary purpose of filtering the incoming traffic between the current network and the source of traffic; this explains the name 'proxy firewall.' Proxy firewalls are transported through a cloud-based tool or a different proxy element. Instead of allowing traffic link up and connect directly, it first identifies a relationship or connection to the origin of traffic and verifies the data packets that come in.

This kind of inspection can be compared to that of a Stateful multilayer inspection firewall because it focuses on both the TCP multiple way handshake protocols and the data packets. Proxy firewalls, however, can also carry out deep-layer packet checks and inspections, verifying the real contents of the information-carrying package to ascertain it has no malware. Upon completion of the check and the data, the packet is given the green light to proceed to the destination; the proxy firewall transfers it off. This procedure builds another layer of gap or separation between the individual devices on operating on your network and the client. This enables them to make another layer of anonymity hence securing your network.

The major advantage of Proxy Firewalls is that they are more secure thanks to the extra layer of anonymity created. They are also pocket-friendly and affordable.

If there is any setback when using proxy firewalls, is that they can slow down the entire internet because they require more steps during the data packet transfer process.

The Software Firewalls

This refers to any firewalls installed on a local device instead of a separate piece of hardware. One of the significant advantages of software firewalls is that they are critical when defensive measures by separating the individual network point end from each other.

One of the significant setbacks of software firewalls, however, is that maintaining them on different sets of devices can be time-consuming and extremely difficult. Additionally, some tools on the network connection may not be compatible with any of the software firewalls. In such occurrences, you will, therefore, have to use various software firewalls for every asset.

Hardware Firewall

This is one of the most popular types of firewalls in the world. The hardware firewall is applied majorly in the modern-day networks as either a LAN network or a border device (used to protect internally placed LAN networks acquired from the internet or any other unwarranted networks) or protecting the internal systems in more significant enterprises. The hardware firewalls mostly have a lot of physical network attributes that can be applied in creating various security zones that are different from Layer 3 elements. Every physical tool can be categorized further into sub-interfaces that, when well propagated, can help expand the secure zones.

When the hardware firewall is operating on its separate hardware application, it can handle vast volumes of data packets as well as millions of network connections. Hardwire firewalls work best in generally high performing machines. The feature that makes the hardware firewall one of the best firewalls to work with is the ability to keep hackers and threats at bay. They are well advanced to alert the administrator of any potential risks and how they can deal with them. Hardware firewalls are, however, more expensive compared to the other firewalls.

Some of the most popular brands that use the hardwire firewall are FortiGate, Checkpoint, Sonic Wall, and Palo Alto.

The Application Firewall

Just as its name goes, the application firewall is a type of firewall that operates at layer seven of the operating system model. Its primary functions are controlling and inspecting the data packets at every application level. This firewall has information about what a typical application should have and that a malicious use contains. It is, therefore, well equipped to filter out any unwarranted access.

For instance, the app firewall that secures a website server has knowledge of the web associated HTTP attacks such as cross-site crippling, and it guarantees the application from such threats by checking into HTTP app traffic. Some of the popular elements that use the application firewall are the Web app firewall. The website app firewall protects the traffic from internet users that come in towards the computer network. Application firewalls are fast gaining popularity thanks to its affordable pricing. It is also one of the most efficient firewalls that help keep threats and hackers at bay.

The Next Generation Firewalls

The next-generation firewall is a term mostly used by manufacturers to refer to a brand of firewalls that are advanced and use high technology standards. What this means is that the next generation firewall combines almost all the firewalls we have discussed above. It is a state of the art kind of firewall that gives application-level inspection and protection.

The next-generation firewall provides comprehensive

analysis and inspection and can locate corrupted traffic in all the layers of the OSI model and any layer associated with it. It contains a host of advanced features, including antivirus features, intrusion detection, and prevention, among others. These features are, however, licensed separately, forcing any interested buyer to spend a little more money to activate all the protections. A good number of next-generation firewalls establish communication using the cloud service security that belongs to the manufacturer to obtain the threat level information from the secure cloud.

What makes next-generation firewalls very efficient is that they have a combination of other features that are well advanced and able to deal with potential threats and incoming hacker detection. The feature that makes the next-generation firewalls one of the best firewalls to work with is the ability to detect security threats even with the slightest detection of malicious activity. They are well advanced to alert the administrator of any system dysfunctions and how they can deal with them. The next-generation firewalls are, however, more expensive compared to the other firewalls. The reason behind this, however, is that they are more advanced and sophisticated compared to any other firewall.

The Stateful Inspection Firewall

A majority of the modern-day firewalls put into use the

feature of tasteful inspection. This might be difficult to understand, and the example highlighted below will help you comprehend it.

In a communication medium between a server and a client (for instance, a person with a website browser engaging in a conversation with a web server), the indicated client browser will initiate an HTTP communication with the server serving the website at port 80. Now assuming that this firewall (the state inspection firewall) allows the HTTP traffic being transferred to pass through it, the data packets will, therefore, be able to reach the servers, which will initiate an instant reply as it is the case with every TCP communication model.

The stateful inspection firewall will store the initiating link that exists between the client, and the server is what is called a state table. The table will have information about details such as the destination IP, the source IP, TCP flags, and the destination ports. This means that any reply coming in from the external web servers that are similar to the connection installed before will have to go through the firewall first then reach the designated servers without the need for extra configuration. The above-mentioned process makes setup easier since the user doesn't have to apply any set of rules on the firewall to reply to the incoming data packets. The data packets mentioned above will instead be allowed automatically only if they are associated with the already installed network connection from the client to the server.

The feature that makes the stateful inspection firewalls one of the best firewalls to work with is the ability to detect security threats even with the slightest detection of malicious activity. They are well advanced to alert the administrator of any system dysfunctions and how they can deal with them. The stateful inspection firewalls are, however, more expensive compared to the other firewalls. The reason behind, however, is that they are more advanced and sophisticated compared to most of the firewalls.

Telephony-Related Firewalls

Just as its name goes, the telephony related firewalls are a type of firewall that operates at layer seven of the operating system model. The primary functions of telephony related firewalls are controlling and inspecting the data packets at every application level. This firewall has information about what a regular application should have and that a malicious use contains. It is, therefore, well equipped to filter out any unwarranted access.

For instance, the app firewall that secures a website server has knowledge of the web associated HTTP attacks such as cross-site crippling, and it ensures the application from such threats by checking into HTTP app traffic. Some of the popular elements that use the application firewall are the Web app firewall.

The website app firewall protects the traffic from internet users that come in towards the computer network. Application firewalls are fast gaining popularity thanks to its affordable pricing. It is also one of the most efficient firewalls that help keep threats and hackers at bay.

Chapter 9: Understanding Cybersecurity

Cybersecurity is the protection of computers' mobile devices, servers, networks, data, and electronic systems from cyber-attacks and malicious viruses. Cybersecurity an also refer to as information technology security. Cyber securities are designed to protect and maintain the confidentiality of the data stored in the internet-connected systems. The organization should have a secure and effective respond to cyber-attacks. The purpose of installing such security measures is to prevent data breaches and identity theft. Cybersecurity is classified into the following categories:

- **Information security**

The protection of data from unauthorized personnel. Goals of securing data protect the confidentiality of the data and preserve the integrity of information either in storage or in transit.

- **Application security**

The procedure of developing, adding, and testing safety features in an application to prevent security attacks against opportunistic malware. A conceded application could make available access to information designed to protect the device. Adequate security always begins at the designing of the app even before the application is installed.

- **Network security**

They are policies and practices implemented to break and monitor accessibility, modification, and misuse of computer or mobile network from unauthorized. The security of the network mostly involves authorizing access of information to authorized persons and usually controlled by the administrator. Network users are assigned by passwords and authority information to access data and programs that are within their security clearance.

- **Operational security**

Operational security includes the processes that recognize and identifies critical information, also determine whether the information, if accessed by malicious individuals, could be useful to them. Operational security also executes and selects a measure that removes any exploitation of helpful information.

- **Disaster recovery and continuity of business**

It is a planning strategy that is capable of restoring data and critical information in inventing that the system was hacked or destroyed during the disaster. When protecting your data, it is good to understand and plan. The plan arises when the application and usage of information after disaster tricks. Continuity of business includes a strategy and action that guarantees that the business will continues after the disaster.

- **End-user education**

The cybersecurity starts with your employees. The end-user is the specific person who uses the hardware device or software program after installation in the machine. Make sure that you educate your employees or yourself on the matter concerning software program or device. The end-user education plays a vital role in keeping the information of the organization safe. The end users are the first line of protection against cyber-attacks.

Importance of Cybersecurity

Cybersecurity considers as most important to an organization, government, institution, and individual. It is essential to protect the family and loved ones from cyber fraud and identity theft. Most of the cyber-attacks happen because of lack of awareness. Cybersecurity has always evolved since the discovery of computers. The modern-day the cyber attackers have improved their tactics in breaking down the systems also installed the internet has improved, making it easier to attack the businesses.

The attackers have developed tools that are designed to exploit the weaknesses of the computer or mobile device. Most hackers do not attack the network, but the website or the server of the organization or individual. Hackers find it difficult to hack the network, as the most network of the organization has a firewall installed hence problematic for them to access. The following are the requirement for cybersecurity:

- Firewall
- Web filtering software
- Endpoint protection
- Intrusion prevention systems
- Radius server
- Logging software
- Encryption

Organizations and businesses can suffer a large amount of money when they fail to safeguard and handle confidential data effectively. There are numerous methods to use to make sure that your data is safe.

An example is hardening, which means that confidential data stored in the corner of a structure, meaning that the information stored inside of a hard shell that cannot be cracked. Placing logging software, any hacker who attempts to access the information in the hardened network will be logged and traced. Installing and using VPNs and encrypted links makes it harder for hackers to access your data. Most hackers will not invest too much to hack into a new security system. It takes time to hack the system, thus increasing the chances of getting caught.

Honeypot is another method of cybersecurity. Placing the right software in the system, any connection that goes in and out of the network can be traced fast. This area of the network is set deliberately and makes the network seem vulnerable. When the hacker attacks the systems, they go straight to the vulnerable area of the net. When they reach there, they steal files and later find out that the data are empty and leave a trace that they were attacking the system.

When cyber network security is secure, the attackers will use a method of social engineering. Social engineering is the method of sending emails telling them to click here. Social engineering has evolved from being told to click here to taking place in internet browsing. Hackers apply the following tactics, phishing, vishing, smishing, and whaling. It is difficult to access the information that was lost since it appears that the data was gladly given. In social engineering, even the smallest mistake of giving out a password to a user account is enough to provide access to hackers to hack data and confidential information about the organization.

Salami cyber-attack hackers steal little money from several banks that lead to a large amount. These attacks can go undetected since the nature of the type of cybercrime.

An electrical protocol should be put in place to detect malware in real-time. The use of heuristic analysis is to observe the behavior of an application or a program to protect it against viruses that change their shape. The organization should train and educate and make them understand their part in keeping the data of the organization protected and report any malicious activity. The organization should put plans in place to deal with any attacks effectively and respond keenly to reduce the impact of the attack on the business.

Data Security Measures and Its Importance

We live in a world where most people use electronic devices & systems in almost every deal and transaction. Technology has resulted in many computer networks and electronic systems, and indeed, they all deal with data. What you might not know is that data one element considered to be very valuable, and internet users are very keen to find out how their information and personal data are handled. Data is, therefore, a precious asset and can have a massive impact on people. It needs severe protective measures to ensure information is secure and brings us to what we shall be discussing in this article: data security and its importance.

What Does Data Security Mean?

Data security refers to the technical process of safeguarding data and keeping it from corrupted and unauthorized access. It isn't all types of data that are essential and sensitive, but others are precious and essential. Having unauthorized people get access to that kind of information can cause a lot of problems because they can use them to do things they are not allowed to do. Data security, therefore, is a defensive measure established to help keep data safe and out of reach for any unauthorized access. There exist a lot of ways you can protect data, as we have discussed below.

The basic concepts of any data security system are confidentiality, integrity, and, lastly, availability. The three concepts are commonly abbreviated as CIA. It is the underlying security model guiding organizations and companies to protect their valuable data from unauthorized people and hackers. Now let's break down each of the concepts and find out what they mean.

- Confidentiality is a concept that makes sure data is available to individuals with authorized access and does not fall in the wrong hands.
- Integrity makes sure that data is accurate and well reliable.
- Availability, on the other hand, is a virtue that makes sure data is readily accessible to serve the needs of clients.

So, what should you consider when setting up data security? Discussed below are some of the essential things you ought to consider when coming up with a security model.

Where is the valuable data placed or located? You can't say

you are protecting something if you have no idea where that thing is put.

The other thing you should consider is who can access your sensitive data? If you have no records of people allowed to access sensitive data, leaves you at high risk if getting accessed by an unauthorized individual. Know who has access to your data because it will give you an idea of the kind of person you are dealing with, and it makes it easier for you to pinpoint any unauthorized access.

Have you actualized the consistent checking and instant alerting on the data? Activating real-time alerts and establishing a continuous monitoring process will ensure the security covers all high alert areas. The real-time alerts play a role in detecting any malicious activity, unwarranted access, and alerts the user before it gets too late.

Below we look at the types of data security, let us discuss some of the technologies used in data security.

Data Security Technologies

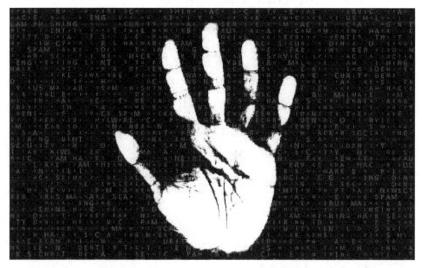

Discussed below are some of the technologies applied in data security today. They are used to reduce the risk involved as well as preventing the security breaches.

- **Data Auditing**

Auditing data when a security breach occurs plays a critical role in preventing it from happening again. Data auditing helps discover essential details of what might have caused the violation. It revealed the people that had access to data during the time of the security breach, how it happened, and the path followed when accessing the file. This kind of technology, therefore, plays a vital role in the process of investigation.

Apart from that, when advanced data auditing solutions are implemented, the information technology administrators can have access to critical visibilities needed to keep unauthorized access at bay.

- **The Real-Time Data Alerts**

In typical situations in today's world, it will take several months for a company to notice they have been breached. One sad fact is that the majority of the companies realize there has been a security breach from their customers or other sources, instead of getting the information their information technology departments.

The real-time data alert technology and constant monitoring of data activity make it easier for you to able to detect security breaches, accidental destruction, as well as unwarranted access to critical personal data.

- **The Data Risk Assessment Technology**

In light of what we have discussed earlier, the data risk assessment technology plays a crucial role in helping organizations know their most vulnerable kind of data and give information about how it can be fixed. The process of doing so starts by identifying the data that is very important and vulnerable, and it can be easily accessible. The risk assessment technology gives a summary of all the found details giving complex feedback on the level of vulnerability and alerts you where you need to work on first.

- **Minimize Data**

During the last ten years of information technology, there has been a significant shift in how people perceive data. In the past, people preferred having more data than less. The more data you had, the more ahead you were.

In today's world, however, data is more of a liability. The potential loss of billions of shillings, securing breach that can destroy the reputation of an entire company as well as the hefty fines associated with collecting more data than what is recommended makes data a very risky asset.

In that connection, it is advised to have only the data you require. Don't ask for people's telephone numbers and home addresses when you only need their identification numbers.

Having learned the data protection technologies, we move on to the types of data protection. Read on to find out!

Types of Data Security

As we have learned earlier, data security protects sensible and vulnerable data from unauthorized access. Almost everything in today's world revolves around computers and the Internet. Music and entertainment transport and infrastructure, healthcare, shopping, and other social aspects have all gone digital. Banks also run their transactions on online platforms. This high dependency on the Internet should make us question the vulnerability of the information and data we have shared. How easily can critical data be accessed without an authorization? Such a question will automatically lead to putting security measures into place.

Discussed below are some of the data security types that can help protect your sensitive data.

- **Critical Security Infrastructure**

This type of data pertains to the advanced cybersecurity systems we rely on in modern society. Let us break it further down and mention a few examples of critical infrastructure: traffic lights, shopping centers as well as the electricity grid. Having any of these vital infrastructures makes it an easy target for unauthorized access and cyber-attacks. For instance, an electricity grid can easily be a target of cyber-attacks.

Therefore, companies and organizations whose data involves the critical infrastructure should put measures in place to protect it from getting in the wrong hands. They need to understand the sensitivity of the information they are handling because it is a critical factor in society's well-being. Additionally, those companies that do not directly deal with critical infrastructure should come with defensive measures to protect it because an attack on could have a significant impact on everyone, including them.

- **The Application Security**

This is one of the must-have data security measures you should consider. It works using the hardware and software techniques to handle impending security threats that can arise towards any sensible data.

Having practical information kept in applications is high risk because they are easily accessible over the Internet, and hackers will access it. Only do so when there are adequate security measures to keep data secured from unauthorized access.

Antivirus programs are some of the application security types. Such protective measures help ensure there is no unauthorized access to data. Additionally, these measures also provide companies that can detect any suspicious activities and puts in place defensive counter attacks.

- **The Network Security**

Having known that data security is more concerned with the threats coming from outside, the network security protects your data from any unauthorized access from people that could have malicious intentions. The network security system keeps data safe by regulating who has access to it and setting security measures; it also detects who has unauthorized access.

With the current technological advances, security measures are getting more sophisticated with the introduction of machine learning to regulate any abnormal traffic as well as detecting threats earlier enough. This type of data protection keeps on implementing procedures and policies that help in preventing unwarranted access and exploitation of data.

Examples of network security implementations include monitored internet access, strong passwords, and software encryption firewalls.

- **The Cloud Security**

The cloud is a result of competent security measures. This is a kind of data security type that is software-based. It monitors and protects data in the cloud resources. Cloud security companies are consistently implementing and developing new cloud security tools that are playing a pivotal role in securing data.

There is a particular myth associated with cloud computing that it is insecure compared to other data security measures. People think that storing your data manually is more secure because you can control it. Research has, however, revealed that storing data in the cloud is safer than storing it physically in a hard disc. It is also easier to control data stored in the cloud.

In 2018, a research carried out by Alert revealed that data stored on-premise receives an average of 62 attacks while data kept in the cloud experiences an average of 25 attacks.

Storing data in the cloud is more secure, saves you the stress of regularly checking on it, and very affordable. It highly recommended using the cloud as your data storage platform. The future is even bright for cloud security thanks to ongoing technological advancements.

- **The IoT (Internet of Things) Security**

Internet of things refers to various critical cyber-physical elements, including printers, Wi-Fi routers, and CCTV cameras. IoT is a type of data security that focuses more on the networks, consumer devices, and other places where data is stored. There exist a lot of IoT devices that are vulnerable to security breaches. This, therefore, needs severe protective measures from all concerned users.

According to research, security is the biggest reason why enterprises hesitate about buying the Internet of things devices. They fear involving it in their business because sensible data might be accessed by unwarranted personnel.

It, therefore, needs everyone's efforts to come up with measures of how data and information can be secured through the Internet of things. Failure to this, we shall be losing critical information and data to unauthorized people who will ruin it.

If your business is run on online platforms, for instance, someone can hack into your system and get your products for free. They can also take your funds and leave you in a financial crisis. This paints the picture of the importance of data security.

Next, we discuss some of the steps you should take when securing data. Read on to find out!

Securing Data

Data security is vital not only for business establishments but for a regular computer user as well. We have discussed the various ways data is essential to us and why we need to secure it. Losing valuable information like bank account details, payment information, as well as client information, can be very difficult to replace. You can imagine the level of damage that can happen if such information falls into the wrongs hands.

Losing data to natural disasters like fires or floods is crushing and mostly uncontrollable, but losing such sensitive data to malware infections or hackers can result in such dire consequences. The good news, however, is that you can control and prevent cybersecurity attacks. Discussed below are the measures you need to take towards safeguarding your data.

- **Assess the Risks**

Any data security measure begins with assessing the levels of risk available. This goes a long way in helping you identify the possible risks and what can be the case if you lost sensitive data through system crash or malware infections.

Below are other threats you are likely to identify during a risk assessment

- o during natural disasters, such as floods, fires, and malicious damage.
- o People authorized to have access to data.

o Identify individuals that regularly use the Internet and e-mail systems in which people are allowed to access sensitive data and those who aren't.

o The use of passwords and how you will maintain them.

o Which kind of firewall and malware solutions are you going to use?

o Educate and sensitize people working with you about what they should do when faced with a security breach.

After carefully analyzing the high potential security threats, go ahead and identify more severe risks and prioritize them. It is also advisable to outline a business continuity plan that your team will use in case of a system breakdown. You likewise frequently check security implementations to ensure they meet the standards of your growing business.

- **Secure Your Data**

After carefully assessing the security threats your data is facing, the next thing should be coming up with defensive measures to prevent that from happening. Given the seriousness of the threats sensitive information faces in the modern world, the best step you can take to keep off intruders should involve a combination of advanced technology, physical preventive tools as well as educated staff. Ensure you are operating on well-defined policies and make your staff is aware of them. Highlighted below are some of the steps you can take towards securing data.

Data security is vital not only for business establishments but for a regular computer user as well. We have discussed the various ways data is essential to us and why we need to secure it. Losing valuable information like bank account details, payment information, as well as client information, can be very difficult to replace. You can imagine the level of damage that can happen if such information falls into the wrongs hands

- o Install alarms and monitoring cameras in your data center or office.
- o Don't allow public access to computers that contain manage sensitive data.
- o Come up with active security measures that will restrict internet access.
- o Always update the anti-malware system. An outdated system is as good as useless.
- o Additionally, ensure the operating system is equipped with the latest features.
- o Prevent hacking attacks by installing intrusion detecting software.
- o Ensure your system has a reliable supply of power.

- **Ensure Mobile Data is Secured**

In today's world, handheld devices have become a popular

way of storing data and communication. It is, however, alarming how data is lost through such devices. Handheld devices are very vulnerable to data theft by getting damaged or being stolen. You, therefore, need to put different measures in place to ensure data is secured and safeguarded. Below are some of the things you can do.

o Always back up your data on removable devices and stored on multiple copies.

o Whenever the device is left somewhere, always activate the password protection.

o When you are in a public place, always ensure you don't leave the device in a home, it can be stolen

o Mobile devices are very fragile; always ensure you protect them from impending physical damage.

It takes a lot of effort to protect data from attacks and cyber threats. It might be costly in some cases, but it is worth every penny. Losing sensitive data to hackers can be something you will never recover from. To protect your data when you can!

Importance of Data Security

From the beginning of the article up to this point, you are now are aware of the significant data carries and why we should protect it. I believe that it has been well tackled. Next, we discuss the importance of data and why it should be kept from falling in the wrong hands. Below are some of the many essential uses of data.

- **Data is liable**

Those of us in the business industry will understand how data is important to us and what it means by calling it an asset. The information regarding the type of products and services provided is essential. In business, for example, you cannot share your strategic plans with and financial objectives with a competitor, they will use it against you, and you will be on the losing end. Other forms of essential data, like client information, are also something precious. It will cost you a lot when such kind of information is breached and finds its way into the hackers. Not only will the clients sue you, but it will also affect the company's image seriously. You are therefore advised to keep information and data secure using the methods we discussed earlier in this article or risk losing it all. Consequently, it needs everyone's efforts to come up with measures of how data and information can be secured through the Internet of things. Failure to this, we shall be losing critical information and data to unauthorized people who will ruin it.

- **It Maintains the Business Reputation**

Almost all kinds of businesses provide products and services to their customers or rather clients. When a customer walks into your business establishments and buys a product or service using the credit card, they trust you with sensitive information. It is, therefore, up to you to keep such sensitive data secure and prevent it from reaching unauthorized personnel. Any kind of security breach, no matter how small that could lead to leaking of information, can have severe damage to the reputation of your business. The client whose data has been leaked might take legal action against your business and trust me; you won't like the consequences. All firms and companies are, therefore, advised to take data security seriously. It will not only impact your business negatively by tainting its reputation but by making you incur extra costs dealing with court proceedings and other legal actions taken against your business.

Chapter 10: Types of Cyber-Attacks and How to Prevent Them

In computing, there are situations where sensitive information may face a threat of access by unwanted people. Computers and computer networks are the critical points where these data can be exploited and used for various reasons. People who gain access to this information usually attempt to steal, benefit, destroy, expose, modify, disable, or control. The access is often unauthorized and targets computer infrastructures, networks, information systems, and private data. This way, cyber-attacks can, therefore, be termed as cyber terrorism or cyber warfare undertaken by individuals, groups, organizations, or society.

A cyber-attack is, therefore, deliberate access to unauthorized information of computer networks, systems, and other technological devices by the use of malicious datasets or codes. The outcome is usually a disruption as well as the compromise of the information resulting in loss of essential data and identity theft, among others. Also referred to as computer network attack, cyber-attacks began in the 1980s and rose over the years. However, measures have been implemented, especially in government and institutional data, to ascertain the security of such information. An attacker, in this case, is an individual, group, or the process of data access to restricted information.

The prevalence of cyber-attacks has become rampant in different regions globally with 2017, seeing the rise of up to two billion stolen data accompanied by a ransomware payment reaching two billion US dollars. Some cyberattacks target private devices, therefore, resulting in identity theft, especially for banks and credit cards. Others focus on user sensitive details to access central databases. On the other hand, the world has also experienced global cyber-attacks where viruses have been planted in computers. Individuals behind such attacks often highlight their demands and provide an antivirus after their conditions are met. As such, there have been multiple types of cyberattacks depending on the attacker and specific data under threat.

Types of Cyber Attacks

Denial of service attacks also includes distributed denial of service, is where the attacker targets the resource system of the computer and makes it unresponsive to service requests. However, the distributed denial of service attack originates from different host machines damaged by malicious software from an attacker. This type of cyber-attack does not necessarily provide direct benefits to the attacker. It only stops the whole process, which may become quite beneficial if the system is of a business competitor. Besides, denial of service attacks may come in handy when an attacker wants to launch an attack hence stops the resource system, including securities and firewalls, and commence an attack.

Denial of service attacks may also come in different forms, TCP SYN flood attack, botnets, ping-of-death, smurf, and teardrop. The TCP SYN flood attack is where the attacker targets Transmission Control Protocols when the system is awaiting connections requests in a queue and becomes unresponsive during the initialization of the connection. Teardrop aims the sequential IP packets by making them overlap, therefore confusing the system and causing it to crash. Smurf attacks use IP spoofing while ping of death focuses on IP packets as well. Botnets, on the other hand, are

173

quite different as they involve millions of computers affected by malware, and the hacker can choose which to attack as he or she has control over all the systems.

Malware Attacks

This is another type of cyber-attack consisting of unwanted software being installed into a computer system without the knowledge of the owner. In most cases, the software is established when an individual is online or has a connection where a hacker can gain access to their computers. More so, malware attacks come in different forms based on where it intends to damage. Most of them attach to original codes and propagate to simulate the application or the internet. Common types of malware attacks include macro viruses, file and system infectors, stealth and polymorphic viruses, logic bombs, Trojans, ransomware, worms, and droppers.

Viruses are the most common malware attack depending on

how they are meant to infect a given system. Macro viruses are specifically intended to affect computer applications, for example, Microsoft Word and Excel, when initialized. Polymorphic viruses focus on encryptions and decryption, especially when using a decryption program, while stealth viruses are responsible for compromising malware detection applications and conceal the scope of an infected file. File and system infectors comprise cyber-attacks that use a virus to infect specific areas within the computer, such as executable codes of files and records in the hard disk.

Trojans are programs that hide within essential system applications but accompany a malicious function. In this case, Trojans allows a hacker to open and gain access to the necessary files without interacting with securities installed. Worms are also a type of malware attack that is commonly transferred by email attachments and activated once the mail is opened. Droppers are another form of malware but used to spread and hide viruses making scanning processes difficult to identify malware. Ransomware is the most dangerous type of malware as it blocks the user from accessing information; therefore, it may be used as a threat to specific demands to be met.

Eavesdropping Attacks

These are cyber-attacks which occur when an attacker

intercepts network traffic and gain access to crucial data such as passwords and other confidential information transferred through the connection. Researchers have categorized eavesdropping into two, active, and passive eavesdropping. Passive eavesdropping entails an attacker monitoring and listening to the message being transferred and learning about it. Active eavesdropping involves a hacker physical disguising as a beneficial party to the user by requesting the message to the transmitter in a process refers to as probing or scanning. Passive eavesdropping is the most dangerous form as they often go unnoticed when compared to active eavesdropping. The best technique to use to avoid eavesdropping attacks is through data encryption.

Cross-Site Scripting Attacks

In some cases, an attacker may use cross-site scripting to gain access to sensitive data through thirty party web resources. That is, the attacker first establishes the targeted information or system and introduces contents consisting of malicious JavaScript in the website database. This malicious program will remain in the database until when the victim opts to requests the webpage. The website will accompany the content with the page embedded within the HTML body to the browser of the victim. When the page completes loading, the malicious script will execute, allowing the attacker to gain access to the computer.

In some instances, the hacker may choose to accompany other vulnerabilities that provide more loopholes to access different areas of your computer. The hacker will then be able to collect all the information needed, including controlling the machine. Cross-site scripting may take various forms, but JavaScript is the most supported and standard used on the web today. Cross-site scripting can, however, affected not only one victim, but also affect others who load similar websites. As to avoid this type of cyber-attack, ensure all the web information is first filtered and validated as well as preventing sending specific information to the resource. Besides, you can disable client-side scripting, making the user have control of the information shared through the web resources.

Password Attacks

Passwords are the most common attacks experienced by victims as they are the sole mechanisms to authenticate the access of user data in specific areas. Acquiring someone's password is most preferably when peeking on their devices or ATMs or other peeks. However, this is not cyber-attacks, as hackers usually gain access to the computer and collect these passwords to open private accounts through computer connections. Like most cyberattacks, password attacks come in different forms and include decryption of passwords, gaining access to the database, outright guessing, and through social engineering.

One of the most common is brute-force password access, which is the guessing of different possible potential words or numbers used as passwords with the intention of one being correct. Another form is through a dictionary attack where a hacker tries to gain access to the connection and computer, and copy the encrypted file and compare it to the dictionary with a similar and possible password format. Some may go ahead and decrypt the password and gain access. One of the primary countermeasures to avoid password attacks is by introducing an account lockout policy that automatically locks after specific password attempts.

Drive-By Attack

These are another common type of cyber-attack where an attacker can readily spread malware through insecure websites. That is, they quickly install malicious script in HTTP or PHP codes in one or more webpages targeting victims who visit these sites. Drive-by scripts may either install the malware into the victim's computer directly or redirect them to the websites of the hacker. In this case, the malware can download immediately the web is loaded or visiting a given website or pop-up pages. This type of cyber-attack does not rely on the user clicking anything or accepting any downloads. This will then enable an attacker to infect your computer without your consent.

When installed into your system, drive-by attacks may infect a program, the operating system as a whole, or browser with security issues. The primary solution for this type of cyber-attack is to keep your computer browser, operating system, and applications updated. You can as well stay away from websites that look suspicious or possess malicious codes essential for causing infections. However, understand that any website can be hacked and compromise the security of your computer. More so, remove any unnecessary or excess applications and programs as they make your device more vulnerable to threats. In other words, the more plugins you have, the more susceptible you are to drive-by cyber-attacks.

Phishing Attacks

Phishing and spear-phishing is the process of sending emails to victims with the aim of gaining access to their personal information or persuade them to do something. The emails are often fake but seem genuine and accompany malware, which quickly loads into your system when you open the attachment. Some useful links to certain websites that lure you into following the instructions given and ending up submitting private data to attackers. The trickery used generally combines social engineering and related techniques to ensure the victim is well influenced to accept to the terms highlighted. Attackers usually have a deeper understanding of their victims, therefore, creating content which suits their personality and relevance.

Identifying these forms of cyberattacks is ordinarily tricky to victims, henceforth finding it hard to defend or resist from handing over crucial data, primarily when a hacker uses email spoofing. Others use website cloning, which commonly fools victims to believe that the emails are legitimate and from trusted sources. There are several ways to reduce and protect yourself from phishing attacks, and one of them is through the use of critical thinking by taking the time to read through and understanding about the sender. Another form is by hovering on the link by deciphering the URL and understands it but never click at first. You can also analyze the headers by learning about the domain and by sandboxing to try and figure out the legitimacy of the mail.

Man-In-The-Middle Attacks

Man-in-the-middle cyber-attacks occur when an attacker gets access between the connection of the victim and server. This type also comes in different forms, which are session hijacking, IP spoofing, and replays. IP spoofing is where the attacker convinces your computer that it is communicating with a genuine entity, therefore, allowing for the access. Similarly, the attacker sends packets with IP source resembling the host instead of the original IP source address making its accept it and act on it. A replay attack is when the attacker impersonates the victim by saving old messages and sending them sooner after the interception. Replays are, however, not valid to hackers as victims can readily prevent them through nonce and timestamps.

Session hijacking is where the attacker intervenes in a session of trusted clients and servers while the primary IP address is substituted, and the server continues with the session. The client first connects to the server, and when the hijacking happens, the attacker gains control by disconnecting the server the client. It then replaces the IP address and continues the sessions with the server as well as the client. With limited countermeasures to man-in-the-middles cyber-attacks, data encryption, and the use of digital certificates may play a significant role in preventing these threats. You should know it is always challenging to understand when an attacker is within a given service; therefore, crucial to forever remain protected against man-in-the-middle cyber-attacks.

SQL Injection Attack

This is a driven-database website attack that occurs when an attacker runs a SQL query within a specific database through the data inputs of a client. The commands are injected in data-planes to execute predefined SQL instructions. When injected successfully, SQL queries access confidential and other sensitive information from the database enabling the attacker to perform the intended purpose. In this case, the data becomes open to the attacker who then can read, change, execute operations, copy, recover and issue commands within the operating system.

For example, a website form may require a user's account name or password, which can be readily be pulled from the database. When such individuals use SQL injections successfully, it allows the information to be drawn from the database and delivered to the attacker at an instant as it already has the details from the victim. The vulnerabilities typically arise due to SQL lacking the ability to differentiate between controls and data planes, thus essential for dynamic SQL, PHP, and ASP. As to protect yourself from this type of cyber-attack, use the least privilege model, which facilitates permissions in your database. This model allows for stable codes that only validate input data of applications through stored procedures and prepared statements.

How to Prevent Cyber Attacks

- **Limit Individuals Accessing Your System**

As already mentioned, among the primary causes of cyberattacks is public use of computer networks and the sharing of communication devices. This has been found to contribute to cyber threats and attacks commonly happening today. As to cub this, you can begin by limiting the number of people accessing your system, especially strangers and uninvited people. You can achieve this by securing your computers by updating software and the use of antiviruses as well as updating the operating system. You can again use company-approved programs and applications rather than purchasing from third parties. This method of prevention is quite useful, especially when you have doubts about people and sources, which tend to cause a threat to your files.

- **Learn About Cyber Attacks**

You can never begin protecting yourself from something you have no idea about how it works; therefore, the need to learn the basics. One of the best ways to do this is through learning about cyber-attacks and become aware of how they operate and harm computers. Having a general knowledge enables you to figure out ways of handling threats and the accompanying attacks when they happen as well as the mitigation measures. This will hence provide exceptional results, especially when you receive emails that you have no idea what they are and go ahead understanding instead of clicking every link you see. Search about facts and continually gain more knowledge with time as attackers also change their tactics over time.

- **Regulate System Infiltration**

Malware is common, and sometimes avoiding them may become a challenge; therefore, continually infect more computers globally. However, you can prevent this type of cyber-attack by readily regulating infiltrations by malware. As to achieve this, ensure any device inserted in your computer is free from any malware such as viruses. You can check it while offline to avoid spreading it through your network. Also, ensure that no third party accesses your computer and enters unknown data as some may plant-specific instructions that allow them to control your system remotely.

- **Enhance Physical Protection**

Other than focusing on online, computer programs, and application security, you should also put in mind the protection of the physical computer itself. Begin by having a lengthy and robust password of not less than eight characters with a mixture of lower and upper letters as well as numbers and symbols. Use identity card authentications where the need is to ascertain your data, especially when providing security to confidential information. Keep all these securities protected at all times without having vulnerabilities that may compromise your cyber-attack security measures.

- **Ghettoize Networks**

Another primary source of computer cyber-attack is through the network, which connects different devices to the server. The host typically has limited threats to your system, but third parties, which are hackers, in this case, may use your connection as an entry point to access your data. Then you have to conceal these loopholes as they contribute to threats of cyber-attacks. One of the practices to do is to prevent other people's devices from accessing private networks by securing stations that facilitate file sharing. Another form is through becoming very cautious, especially on what you share online, as some information you share may be used against you. Besides, ensure that you avoid using public networks with devices that consist of critical and sensitive data as most hackers may take advantage and benefit from your mistake.

- **Constantly Update Your Securities**

Most often, the best way to prevent cyber-attacks is to ensure that your system is full of all applications, software, and programs that facilitate the needed protection. What many fail to understand is that cyber-attacks, especially for malware change over time, and if you fail to make an update, your securities may fail to protect the system. In this case, the best way to handle these attracts is by ensuring that antiviruses, antispyware, firewalls, and software in the operating system are updated. Make these updates regularly to ensure you have the more recent version of your securities. You should be aware that hackers also understand this, and any delays in making updates may cost you. As such, ensure that you quickly make the updates as soon as they are available.

Hacking
with
Kali Linux

A Comprehensive Guide for Beginners to Learn Basic Hacking, Cybersecurity, Wireless Networks, and Penetration Testing

By Dylan Mach

information contained within this document, including, but not limited to, — errors, omissions, or inaccuracies.

Table of Contents

Introduction

Congratulations on purchasing *Hacking with Kali Linux,* and thank you for doing so.

The following chapters will discuss all of the different parts that we need to know more about when it is time to work with the idea of hacking and working with Kali Linux in order to get this all done. There are a lot of different tools that we are able to utilize when it comes to hacking, but one of the very best operating systems that we are able to use to make this into a reality is the Kali Linux system. This guidebook is going to take some time to go through all of that and learn more about how we can make it all work.

The start of this guidebook is going to take a look at some of the basics of hacking, the reasons that we would want to spend some time looking at hacking and using it for our own networks, and a good look at the difference between ethical hackers, unethical hackers, and everyone in between.

From there, we are going to take a look at a bit about cybersecurity and cyber attacks. With our modern world and the fact that so many people are online and trying to share and look at information all of the time, it is no wonder that hackers are trying to find methods that will allow them to get onto the computers and networks out there to steal personal and financial information any time that they would like. That is why we are going to take some time to look at how we can keep our networks safe and secure with cybersecurity while also knowing which types of cyber attacks are the most likely.

Now it is time to take this a bit further and look more at how hacking is going to work. We are going to take a look at the hacking process in more details, while also looking at malware, and how that, and a few other types of attacks are going to be able to come into play to help us really see results.

Then it is time to move on to some of the things that we are able to do with the Kali Linux system. This is often considered one of the best coding operating systems to work with, and we are going to take the time to look at what it is about and how we are able to use it for our needs. In this part, we are going to look at the reasons that people like to work with Linux, how to set up Kali Linux, how to work with Kali in a Virtual Machine if this is the best option for us, and even how to organize Kali Linux, so it is ready for some of the attacks that we want to do.

This is just the beginning of what we are able to do when it comes to hacking. Now that we have set the stage and we are all ready to go with some of this, it is time to take it a bit further and look at some of the neat things that we can use Kali Linux to help us out with. We are going to look at how to scan and manage our networks, the importance of firewalls, how to obtain user information when we want, the use of Kali Linux on some of the portable devices we want to use, and even how to work with MalDuino and Kismet.

This is not all, though. We are going to take a look at a few more of the steps that we are able to work with when it is time to hack a network of our choice and gather up the information that we would like. To finish out this guidebook, we are also going to spend some time looking at how we are able to bypass a hidden SSHS, how to hack onto the WPA and WPA2 wireless systems, how to use some of the different tools out there to make sure that you stay hidden and no one will be able to trace the attacks back to you, and how we are able to use Metasploit to help us complete our own penetration testing.

As we can see with this guidebook, there are a ton of different parts that need to come into play so that we can really complete the attack that we would like to work with. All of these are different methods that hackers, those who are brand new and those who have been in the game for some time, are able to do. When you are looking to protect your own network or the network for someone else, or you would like to hack onto another network, you will be happy that you have all of these tools ready to help you get this work done.

There are a lot of cool things that we are able to do when it is time to work with the process of hacking, and having this all prepared and ready to go can be one of the best methods you can choose to protect your own network. When you are ready to learn more about hacking and all of the tools and techniques that we are able to use when hacking along with the Kali Linux system, make sure to check out this guidebook to get started.

There are plenty of books on this subject on the market, thanks again for choosing this one! Every effort was made to ensure it is full of as much useful information as possible; please enjoy!

Chapter 1: Definition of Hacking and Types of Hackers

The process of hacking involves getting unauthorized access into a computer system, or a group of computer systems. Hackers get access to systems by cracking codes or passwords. The technique hackers use to obtain code or password is cracking and a hacker is someone that undertakes the process of hacking. Hackers can hack an email account, a social media site, a website, an entire LAN network, or a group of systems. Ultimately, it is through password algorithms programs that the hackers obtain access to a password.

For each of their daily needs, people and also businesses make use of laptops or computers. For a seamless flow of business applications and information, several organizations

200

have WAN, wide area network, website or domain, or a computer network. As a result, there is a high-risk exposure of these networks to hackers as well as the outside world of hacking.

Purpose of Hacking

Mostly, the objective of some hackers is to cause certain reputational or financial harm to an entity, group, or person through their malicious or criminal intent. They achieve this by spreading malicious or incorrect rumors that can cause the disruption of the business after they embezzle their funds or steal their confidential data. Companies can find themselves in some socially detrimental situations with this misleading information. Also, as punishable by law, hacking is a form of internet or cybercrime. However, government law agencies and specific accredited institutions engage in another side of hacking on a professional level. With this case, their intention is to prevent individuals from causing any harm or counter the wrong intentions of the hackers. Also, this type of hacking is done to protect and save the citizens and society at large.

Types of Hackers

It is quite essential for us to differentiate between the objectives and roles of hackers by knowing their types to get the detail on the above-broached objectives.

Hacktivist

Leaving contentious information on a website that they hack is the focus of these types of hackers. They do this to spread religious, social, and political messages. Also, other nations can be targeted by these hackers.

Grey hat

These types of hackers have no intention of fraudulent when they access a system without any authorization. They are between the black and white hat hackers. The objective of these hackers is to show the stakeholders of the system parts of its weaknesses and vulnerabilities.

Ethical Hacker

The objective of these types of hackers is to eliminate and identify suspected weaknesses. They assess systems by getting access as officially and recognized stamped hackers and they are known also as white hat. A few things they also do is to retrieve critical information needed for security purposes, crack codes of anti-social or illegal setups, and vulnerability assessment. They are paid, certified, and trained experts.

The ethical hackers are the only individuals who are allowed to do this kind of hacking legally. They know the same kinds of rules to follow as a black hat hacker and will use some of the same ideas along the way. But they have usually gained permission to go through and do some of these options, rather than trying to do it to gain their own personal advantage.

For the ethical hacker, the goal is to keep the system as safe and secure as possible along the way. They want to either protect their own network, or the network of someone else who knows what they are here. This will make it easier for them to get onto the network without doing so in an illegal manner.

These hackers are going to use a lot of the same methods for their attacks, as we see with some of the other types of hackers. This means that they are going to rely on penetration testing, mapping out attacks, and more. But they are going to do it as a way to help them figure out where the vulnerabilities in the system are rather than looking at ways that you can exploit them.

Cracker

These are black hat. They secure entry into websites or computer networks through an unauthorized manner and also with a mala fide intention. There is also an attachment of personal gain in their intention through privacy rights violations to benefit criminal organizations, stealing of funds from online bank accounts, stealing confidential organizational information, and so on. These days, these hackers engage in their activities in a shady manner and they belong to this category.

Types of Hacking

The threats that websites have to deal with are some of the most frequent threats of hacking. Hackers engage in the process of making the contents of a website public or changed with the use of unauthorized access. The individuals or groups that are opposed to social or political organizations most times target their websites. Also, they hack national or governmental information website, and this is entirely common. Here are some of common the hacking methods they use on the websites:

DNS Spoofing

Sometimes, users might forget about the cache data of a domain or website, and this method of hacking uses this cache data. Then, it points the data to another malicious website.

Cookie Theft

Cookies contain login passwords, confidential information,

and so on, and with the use of malicious codes, hackers will have access to the website to steal cookies. When a legitimate company uses these, it is going to help them provide you with a better service overall. But it does store a lot of extra information on you and your system, and if the hacker is able to steal these cookies, they will be able to use them in any manner that they would like. This could be dangerous and is a big reason that it is often best to turn off and disable the use of cookies in the first place.

UI Redress

Hackers use this method by creating a fake user interface. Thus, users will be directed to another website altogether when they click with the intention of going to a specific site.

Virus

When hackers get access to a specific website, they release a virus into the files of the website. Their objectives are to corrupt the resources or information on such a website. There are a lot of different types of viruses that we are able to meet up with, and they can be spread through email attachments, websites that have been compromised, and more.

These viruses can take over the computer, shutting down files, stealing information, and even spreading to some of the contacts that you have on your system to get the information that the hackers would like to have. This is why it is so important to go through and be careful about the kinds of websites that you open, and to make sure that you are not going to websites that could harm your computer.

Phishing

They use this method to replicate the original website, and as such, the hackers will easily seize and misuse the unsuspecting user's information like credit card details, account password, and so many more.

Many times these are going to be sent through email. The email is going to appear as it comes from the legitimate source, such as your bank or another site that you spend some time on, asking for you to check out a message or change your username and password.

Because the hacker does a great job of hiding things and making it look official, it does not take that long for people to fall for it. Even the website is going to look legitimate so it is easy to click on the different items and enter the information. If someone does fall for this, the hacker is able to take all of that information and use it to actually get into the account of yours that they would like.

How Do Hackers Get Access into Computer Systems

We can get information by working and communicating with others through the help of some good guys in the computer world that create networks. And then, for a variety of reasons, we have some not-so-good individuals that cause troubles by using their computers to worm their way into those networks. These set of individuals are hackers and part of the things they engage in include:

- Shut down a website by creating heavy traffic to it
- Obtain credit card information
- Get passwords
- Steal secrets

Whether by disrupting business as usual or stealing information for their gain, hackers are always at work. Every now and then, there will always be news about them, and at a point, you may likely be wondering about just exactly what hackers are doing. They are always getting in the system by stealing passwords. For them to crack the security of a network, the first step for them is to find out a password. As a result, to make your password hard to figure out by anyone, it is quite useful to change them regularly. For you to know what hackers do when people discuss them, here are some key terms that you may probably hear about them:

- **Trojan horse**: this technique appears to be a helpful program and users are tricked into clicking and opening it. But the computers of such users can get unexpected attacks which can be behind the scenes or unnoticed. Because these are going to sneak onto the computer through methods that are secret, such as being on a program that seems legitimate, it is hard to detect them. But when the Trojan horse gets into the system, it can open up back doors and other things to help the hacker get the information that they want.
- **Session hijacking**: this technique involves hackers inserting malicious data packets into an actual data transmission over the internet connection.
- **Script kiddie**: this is unsophisticated or young hackers who act like a real hacker while using hackers' tools. These individuals are not going to care that much about learning how to hack. They want to complete an attack, but they don't really care about the basics that go with it or the codes that they need to use. Instead, they are going to just take on some of the tools and programs that are already out there and will use these to help them out. They just want to complete the hack and get the information out of it, without having to worry about learning any of the techniques along the way.
- **Root kit**: an intruder can disguise and expand his control over your system by using this set of tools.
- **Root access**: for any hacker to get complete control over a system, root access is the highest level of access. Root access is the most desired by serious hackers to a computer system.

- **Email worm**: hackers use a natural-looking email message to send a mini-program or virus-laden script to an unsuspecting victim.
- **Denial-of-service attack**: hackers use this method to flood a website with false traffic, thereby preventing the system of the victim or crippling it from handling its normal traffic. This one is going to turn down the server for a particular company and can make it hard for legitimate users to get onto the system at all. This allows the hacker to have a chance to leave a Trojan or a back door or something else on that network.
  - **Distributed Denial of Service**: This one is going to be a bit different because it is going to utilize more than one computer to do the attack. In the DoS, the hacker is just using one computer, and the firewall can usually see that IP address and will stop allowing the service from that address. With the DDoS, the hacker is using a lot of different computers to do the process which makes it harder for the firewall to stop the attack.
- **Buffer overflow**: hackers use this method by overrunning an application buffer to deliver malicious commands to a system.
- **Back door**: hackers get access to a computer system using this secret pathway. Trojan horses, viruses, and other types of malware are able to come in and utilize this option to help them get onto the system and come back and forth as many times as they would like. If you are trying to protect your own computer or another system, make sure that when you are all done, you fix it all up so there are no potential back doors for a hacker to get through.

Guarding Against Hacking

A persistent threat that is continuously affecting the security of a nation and its citizens is hacking. At the level of the individual, when hackers wipe away the entire hard-earned financial savings of someone, it can result in untold financial losses. Also, it can lead to long-term repercussions and major financial losses through the theft of data at the organizational level. It is essential to block this vicious menace and safeguard it.

There are a lot of things that you are able to do to make sure that you can keep your own network safe against another hacker. Setting this up well, and being careful about how your own network is going to behave is going to be so important to keep the hackers out. Some of the different steps that you are able to take in order to guard against any hackers that would like to get on your network will include:

1. Be careful about the emails that you use. Many of the attacks that we are going to explore in this guidebook are going to be activated with the help of email. This isn't true all of the time. But if you are careful with some of the emails that you open, especially the attachments, then you can avoid a lot of these attacks from a hacker.

2. Pick out some strong passwords that are harder to guess or get through with a brute force attack. Pick out passwords that are long, use a combination of letters, numbers and symbols, and ones that are not going to be related back to you or easy to guess at all. Many hackers are going to start by trying to attack your passwords because this is a weak point in your security. You can ix this with the help of a strong password.

3. Do a penetration test to look for some of the vulnerabilities that are on the system. We will take a look at how to work with penetration testing later on, but this is a great way to figure out which places the hacker may try to use in order to get onto your network. Doing one for yourself will help to keep it protected.

4. Change passwords on a regular basis. When you change the password on a regular basis, it is a lot harder for the hacker to guess what it is or use some of the other methods of password cracking to get through with the help of the password.

5. Do not share information about the network with anyone else. Any important and sensitive information about your network needs to be kept secret and hidden. The more people who know about your

network, the more likely it is that the information will get out, and a hacker will be able to utilize this.

6. Consider encrypting the information that you send to others in your communications. This makes it hard for anyone who does not have the right key to read any of the information that you are sending, even if it does get intercepted.

7. Pick out a strong security protocol to protect your network. Make sure that you are not working with the WEP option because this one is often easier for a hacker to get through. While the WPA and WPA2 are still options that are vulnerable to an attack, they are a lot stronger and can keep you safer along the way.

8. Use anti-malware and anti-virus software. These will make it harder for any of the attacks that the hacker is trying to send your way to get through.

9. Make sure that you are updating your software and operating system as often as it is needed. These updates are going to help cut out some of the vulnerabilities that are found in the operating system you use, and other software, so doing the update will make it harder for a hacker to get onto your system.

As you can see, there are going to be a lot of options that you are able to work with when it is time to protect your computer compared to some of the hacks that are coming your way. Make sure to work with some of these options, and you will find that it is a lot harder for a hacker to get on your system and use it for their own advantage along the way.

Chapter 2: Cybersecurity

The practice of defending data, networks, electronic systems, mobile devices, servers, and computers from malicious attacks is cybersecurity. Also, they refer to it as electronic information security or information technology security. Common categories can also fit into the terms as well as a variety of contexts, from mobile to business computing.

- The most unpredictable cybersecurity factor is end-user education. When people fail to follow healthy security practices, they can accidentally introduce a virus to an otherwise secure system. Thus, it is quite vital for the security of any organization to educate its employees not to plug in unidentified USB drives and to delete suspicious email attachments.

- For any causes of loss of data or operations, the manner with which an organization responds to a cybersecurity incident is the business continuity and disaster recovery. And for the organization to return to the same operating capacity as before the event, the processes that dictate how the organization restores its information and operation are the disaster recovery policies. While the organization is attempting to operate without specific resources, the organization has a plan that it falls back on, which is the business continuity.

- The decisions and procedures of protecting and handling data assets are operational security. This process encompasses the activities that determine where and how data may be shared or stored and the users' permissions while accessing a network.
- When data is in transit or in storage, the privacy and integrity of data are protected by the information security.
- For devices and software to be free of threats is the focus of the application security. Even though it is designed to protect data, a compromised application could provide access to the data. Before the deployment of a device or program, the design phase is the beginning of the successful security.
- Irrespective of if an attack may come from opportunistic malware or targeted attackers, the practice of securing a computer network from intruders is the network security.

Cyber Threat Scale

Every year, about $19 billion is spent by the U.S. government on cybersecurity. However, the pace at which the cyber-attacks are evolving is quite fast. According to NIST, the National Institute of Standards and Technology, real-time monitoring of all electronic resources is recommended to aid in early detection and combat the proliferation of malicious code. Cybersecurity counter three-fold threats and they are:

1. To cause fear or panic, the intention of cyberterror is to undermine electronic systems
2. Most times, politically motivated information gathering is involved in cyber-attacks
3. For financial gain or to cause disruption, groups or single actors can target systems through cybercrime.

Ransomware, Trojans, spyware, worms, and viruses are some of the common techniques attackers utilize to control networks or computers. For surreptitious data collection, they make use of Trojans and spyware and to damage or self-replicate systems or files. They use worms or viruses. All the information of the user is encrypted by ransomware, who waits for an opportunity to do so, and for the use to get access to their encrypted information, there will be demands for payment. A legitimate-looking download can contain a malware payload and they use it and also unsolicited email attachment to spread malicious code.

Irrespective of size, all industries have their fair share of the cybersecurity. In recent years, government, finance, manufacturing, and healthcare are some of the industries that reported the most cyberattacks. Since these industries collect medical and financial data, several of these sectors are more appealing to cybercriminals. However, they can also target all businesses that use networks for customer attacks, corporate espionage, and customer data.

More than before, the world relies on technology. As such, there is a surge in digital data creation. Today, computers are used to store a great deal of that data by governments and businesses, and they transmit it across networks to other computers. There is vulnerability in devices and their underlying systems that undermine the objectives and health of an organization when exploited. For any business, there can be a range of devastating consequences with a data breach. Through the loss of partner and consumer trust, a data breach can unravel the reputation of a company. A company can lose its competitive advantage through the loss of vital data such as intellectual property or source files. Also, because of non-compliance with data protection regulations, corporate revenue can be impacted through a data breach. About $3.6 million is the average cost that a data breach can cost an affected organization. It is quite critical for organizations to implement and adopt a strong cybersecurity approach with high-profile data breaches making media headlines.

Advancement of Cybersecurity

The focus of traditional cybersecurity is on the implementation of defensive measures around a defined perimeter. BYOD, Bring Your Own Device and remote workers are the recent enablement initiatives that have expended the attack surface, reduced the visibility into cyber activity, and dissolved the perimeter. Today, despite the record levels of security spending, there is a rapid increment in breaches. The focus is on human-centric cybersecurity for a global organization. It is a new approach that, instead of an exponential number of growing threats, places focus on changes in user behavior. Where data resides, human-centric cybersecurity extends security controls into all the systems and also offers insight into the manner with which an end-user interacts with data even when the organization is not in control exclusively. Ultimately, to reduce threat detection and investigation times as well as prioritize and surface the most serious threats, this approach is designed to identify behavioral anomalies.

Protecting the End-User

So, what are the security measures provided by cybersecurity for systems and users? First, to encrypt files, emails, and other vital data, cybersecurity relies on cryptographic protocols. Not only does this technique guard against theft or loss, but it also protects information in transit. Also, the computer is scanned by the end-user security software for pieces of malicious code, quarantines this code, and then deletes it from the system. For malicious code hidden in MBR, Master Boot Record with a specific design to wipe or encrypt data from the hard drive of computers, security programs can also remove them after it has detected them. There is also a focus on real-time malware detection by electronic security protocols. For some to monitor the behavior of a program and its code to defend against Trojans and viruses that change their shape with each execution, both metamorphic and polymorphic malware, they make use of behavioral analysis and heuristic. From the network of a user, security programs can confine potentially malicious programs to a virtual bubble to learn how to better detect new infections and analyze their behavior. And as experts of cybersecurity identify new ways to combat new threats, security programs continue to evolve new defenses.

Chapter 3: Types of Cyber Attacks

With the use of several techniques to destroy, alter, or steal information or data systems, any targeted offensive action that focuses on personal, computer devices, infrastructures, or computer information systems is a cyberattack. Without further ado, here are some of the common cyberattacks today:

Birthday Attack

The creation of the birthday attacks is developed against hash algorithms which people use to confirm the integrity of a digital signature, software, or a message. A fixed length MD, message digest, which is independent of the input message length, is produced by a processed hash function message.

The message has the characteristics of this MD uniquely. The probability of finding two random messages is the reference for the birthday attack, which, when processed by a hash function, generates the same MD. The attacker can safely replace the message of the user with his if the attacker calculates a similar MD for the message as the user has. And even if they compare MDs, the receiver will not be able to detect the replacement.

Eavesdropping Attack

Attackers intercept the network traffic for the eavesdropping attack to happen. For some confidential information that a user might be sending over the network such as credit card numbers and passwords, an attacker can obtain those data by eavesdropping. There are two types of eavesdropping attackers, and they are active and passive:

- Active eavesdropping: by sending queries to transmitters, the attackers will disguise themselves as friendly units as they actively grab the information. They call this process as tampering, scanning, or probing.
- Passive eavesdropping: when attackers listen to the message transmission in the network, they will detect the information.

Also, since by conducting passive eavesdropping before active attacks require the attacker to gain knowledge of the friendly units, quite essential than spotting active ones is detecting passive eavesdropping attacks. To guard against eavesdropping, the best countermeasure is data encryption.

XSS, Cross-Site Scripting Attack

For running scriptable applications or scripts in the web browser of the victim, it is the third-party web resources that the XSS attacks use. Essentially, the attacker will use malicious JavaScript by injecting a payload into the database of a website. Using the payload of the attacker as part of the HTML body, the website will transmit the page to the browser of the victim to execute the malicious script when the victim requests a page from the website. For example, the attacker can use the cookie from the server of the attacker after extracting it for session hijacking when it sends this cookie of the victim. When they use XSS to exploit more vulnerability, there can be the most dangerous consequences. Attackers can control and access the machine of the victim remotely, collect as they discover network information, capture screenshots, or log keystrokes in addition to stealing cookies through these vulnerabilities. Since there is a wide support for JavaScript on the web, it is the most widely abused while, within Flash, ActiveX, and VBScript, they can take advantage of XSS.

Data input can be sanitized by the developers when users in an HTTP request before reflecting it back to defend against XSS attacks. And before echoing back anything to the user, it is essential to see that all data is escaped, filtered, and validated, including the values of query parameters during searchers. Special characters like >, <, /, &, ?, spaces can be converted to their respective URL encoded equivalent of HTML. Users can have the option of disabling client-side scripts.

SQL Injection Attack

For websites that are database-driven, one common issue is the SQL injection. The process happens when, from client to server, a malefactor executes a SQL query to the database through the input data. In order to run predefined SQL commands, it is possible to insert SQL commands into data-plane input, for example, instead of the password or login.

From the database, sensitive data can be exploited by a successful SQL injection. Also, it can issue commands to the operating system, recover the content of a given file, execute administration operations like shutdown on the database, and also modify (delete, update, or insert) database data. For example, the account of a user can be requested by a web form on a website and then to pull up the connected account information using dynamic SQL, send it to the database. The process can leave a hole for attackers even when this works for users who are properly entering their account number.

There is no specific distinction between the data and control planes with the vulnerability to this type of cybersecurity attack. Thus, if a site utilizes dynamic SQL, SQL injections can work mostly. Also, because of the prevalence of older functional interfaces, SQL injection is quite common with ASP and PHP applications. And due to the availability of the programmatic interface nature, the less likely easily exploited SQL injections are ASP.NET and J2EE. In your database, apply the leastoprivilege model of permission to protect yourself from a SQL injection attacks. It is vital not to include any dynamic SQL as you adhere to the process and parameterized queries for the prepared statements. And to prevent injection attacks, you will require a strong database for the executed code. Also, at the application level, it is vital to validate input data against a white list.

Password Attack

Obtaining passwords tend to be the effective and common attack approaches since to authenticate users to an information system, passwords are the most commonly used mechanism. Through outright guessing, gaining access to a password database, using social engineering, acquiring unencrypted passwords by sniffing the connection to the network, or looking around the desk of a person, attackers can get access to the password of a person. Then, they can use a systematic or random manner to execute the last approach.

- Using the **dictionary attack**, attack attempts to gain access to the network or computer of a user by using a dictionary of common passwords. Attackers may compare the results after applying similar encryption to a commonly used password dictionary as they copy an encrypted file that contains the passwords.

- Attackers may hope that one password will work after using a random approach to guess different passwords. This process is called **Brute-force**. The process tends to be logical for attackers when they use hobbies, title, job, name, and similar terms of the person to guess passwords related to the person.

An account lockout policy that will lock your account after some invalid password attempts is all that is needed to protect yourself from brute-force and dictionary attacks.

Drive-By Attack

The prevalent technique to spread malware is the drive-by download attacks. On one of the pages, attackers will have a malicious script planted into PHP or HTTP code. With this planted, the script could redirect the victim to a site controlled by the hackers or might install malware directly onto the visitor's computer. When viewing or visiting a pop-up window or an email message or when you are visiting a website, drive-by downloads can take place. You can be infected with a drive-by attack even if you don't open a malicious email attachment or click on a download button. For you to enable the attack, you may not necessarily have to do anything, which makes drive-by attack different from other kinds of cybersecurity attacks. Due to a lack of updates or unsuccessful updates, a drive-by download can take advantage of a web browser, operating system, or an app that contained security flaws.

You may be required to avoid websites that could contain malicious code and keep your operating systems or browsers up to date to guard yourself against drive-by attacks. Even though those websites are liable to hacking, try to stick to the sites you use normally. And always delete unnecessary apps or programs from your device. Drive-by attacks can exploit more vulnerability on your system when you have more plug-ins.

Phishing and Spear Phishing Attacks

The purpose of a phishing attack is to influence users to do something or gain personal information by sending an email that seems to originate from trusted sources. This type of attack utilizes technical trickery and social engineering. Malware can be loaded into your computer through an attachment of an email. Also, you can be tricked into handing over your personal information or downloading the malware through a link to an illegitimate website. A phishing activity that is quite targeted is spear phishing. A bit of research goes into the targets by the attacker, after which relevant and personal messages are created. Spear phishing appears to be quite hard to be identified and guarding against it can also be harder. Email spoofing is one of the simplest approaches hackers use to conduct a spear-phishing attack. They make the email seem like it is coming from a known person like your partner or management since they have falsified the information in the section "From" of the email. Also, website cloning is another method that scammers use to infuse credibility to their story. They will fool you to enter login credentials or personally identifiable information, PII.

Here are some methods you can engage in cutting down on

the risk of phishing:

- **Sandboxing**: you can make use of a sandbox environment to test the content of the email, clicking the links inside the email, or logging activity from opening the attachment
- **Email header analysis**: how an email got to your address is the purpose of email headers. As is stated in the email, there must be similarity in the domain of the "Return-Path" and the "Reply-to" parameters.
- **Hovering over the links**: don't attempt to click it when you move your mouse over the link. You will know where it will actually take you when you hover your mouse over the link, and to decipher the URL, you will need to apply critical thinking.
- **Critical thinking**: just because you have 200 other unread messages in your inbox or you are stressed or busy, you will take it that an email is the real deal. You will want to take a minute to analyze the email.
-

MitM, Man-in-the-Middle Attack

In the situation where a hacker plants itself between a server and the communications, a MitM attack is happening. Some of the man-in-the-middle attack types include:

Replay

Attackers can impersonate one of the participants by intercepting and saving old messages and attempt to send them later; thereby, a replay attack is taking place. You can use a string that changes later or a random number to counter which nonce or session timestamps to easily counter it.

IP Spoofing

IP spoofing happens when a system provides the attacker with access to it, thinking that it is communicating with a trusted, known entity. A target host gets a trusted, known host from the attacker who, instead of its own IP source address, sends a packet with such an IP source. It is possible for the target host to act upon it after accepting the packet.

Session Hijacking

Between the network server and a trusted client, attackers can hijack a session in this type of MitM attack. While the belief of the server is that of a communication with the client as it continues the session, there will be a substitution of the IP address of the attacking computer for the trusted client. For example, the process of the attack can go thus:

1. There is a connection by the client to a server.
2. The client's control is gained by the computer of the attacker.
3. The computer of the attacker disconnects the client from the server.
4. The attacker uses their IP address to replace that of the IP address of the client, thereby, spoofing the sequence numbers of the client.

5. There is a continuous dialog by the computer of the attacker with the server, and the belief of the server is that the communication still continues with the client.

For the prevention of all MitM attacks at present, there is no configuration or single technology to do the magic. Overall, effective safeguards against MitM attacks are digital certification and encryption, with both assuring integrity and confidentiality of communications. However, that encryption might not help with the way attackers will inject a man-in-the-middle attack. For example, the public key of a man named Greg may be intercepted by an attacker and as such, makes the substitution of that key as his key. Then, anyone could unknowingly use the substituted public key by the attacker, thinking they are sending an encrypted message to Greg. Therefore, the intended message for Greg can be read by the attacker and then uses the genuine Greg's encrypted key to send the message to Greg, and Greg will never notice that the message has been compromised. Also, before sending the message to Greg, the attacker can modify the message. Ultimately, because of the MitM attack, Greg will believe that his information is protected since he is using encryption.

Now, how do you distinguish between the ownership of the public key between the two of them? Solving such a problem like this instigates the development of hash functions and certificate authorities. The following technique can be utilized when someone wants to be sure that an attacker will not see a message they want to send to Greg and that the message will indeed come from that message without any modification from an attacker:

1. A symmetric key will be encrypted by the person after they have created it with their own public key.
2. Then, the person will forward the encrypted symmetric key to Greg.
3. After that, the person will digitally sign a hash function of the message that they have computed.
4. Then, with the use of the symmetric key, the person will encrypt the signed hash message and their message and then sends forward the whole thing to Greg.
5. Since only Greg has the private key to decrypt the encryption, Greg will be able to receive the symmetric key from the person.
6. Since he has the symmetric key, the only person that can decrypt the symmetric signed hash and encrypted message is Greg.
7. And because Greg can compare the received message's hash with digitally signed one and can compute the hash of the received message, Greg can confirm that the message has not been altered.
8. Since only the person can sign the hash for it to verify with the person's public key, Greg can also prove to himself that the person was the sender.

DoS, Denial-of Service, and DDoS Distributed Denial-of-Service Attacks

When the resources of a system cannot respond to service requests, it means a denial-of-service attack has overwhelmed such a system. Though, the attacker controls the malicious software that they have infected in a large number of other host machines, the attack of a DDoS is also on the resources of a system. Attackers don't gain direct benefit from denial-of-service, unlike attacks that they developed to increase or gain access. DoS attacks satisfy some of the attackers. However, there may be real enough benefits for attackers if the attacked resources belong to a business competitor. Also, for attackers to launch a new type of attack, they tend to result in DoS attacks to take a system offline. Here are some of the various kinds of DDoS and DoS attacks:

Botnets

For hackers to implement DDoS attacks, they can inflect millions of systems with malware using botnets. And to carry out the attacks against the target systems, they use these bots or zombie systems. Most times, these will overwhelm the processing capacity and bandwidth of the target system. And since the locations of the botnets are quite differing, it can be difficult to trace these DDoS attacks. The mitigation of botnets can arise through:

- Using black hole filtering. Before it enters a protected network, it drops undesirable traffic. The host of the Border Gateway Protocol is required to forward routing updates to ISP routers in the event of detecting a DDoS attack. At the next hop, null0 interface will receive all traffic heading to victim servers.
- To deny traffic from spoofed addresses, using RFC3704 filtering, which its correct source network can be traced for that traffic. For example, from bogon list addresses, packets will be dropped by RFC3704 filtering.

Ping of Death Attack

Ping of death attacks makes use of an IP size over the maximum of 65,535 bytes to ping a target system using IP packets. The IP packet is fragmented by the attackers since IP packets of this size are not allowed. Then, other crashes can ensue as well as buffer overflow when the target system reassembles the packet. When you use a firewall, you can block the attack of the ping of death as the IP packets that have been fragmented will be checked for maximum size.

Smurf Attack

Attackers saturate a target network with traffic with the ICMP as well as using IP spoofing with this attack. Attackers target the broadcast IP addresses with the use of ICMP echo requests. As such, the origin of these ICMP requests is from the address of a spoofed victim. For example, for the attackers to broadcast address 10.255.255.255, the attacker would spoof an ICMP echo request from 10.0.0.10 if the intended victim address is 10.0.0.10. All IPs in the range will get this request, and it would overwhelm the network since all the responses are going back to 10.0.0.10. Not only can this method generate a vast amount of network congestion, but it can also be automated as it can be repeatable. You may want to disable IP-directed broadcasts at the routers for you to protect your devices from this attack. Then, you will be able to protect the ICMP echo broadcast request at the network devices. Also, to keep them from responding to ICMP packets from broadcast addresses, another option is to configure the end systems.

Teardrop Attack

Attackers use this method to offset fields in sequential Internet Protocol packets by causing the fragmentation and length to overlap one another on the attacked host. Though it will fail, during the process, there will be an attempt by the attacked system to reconstruct packets. Then, the system will crash eventually due to confusion. You may want to block ports 445 and 139 as you disable SMBv2 for you to protect against this DoS attack if you don't have patches.

TCP SYN Flood Attack

It is during a TCP session initialization handshake when attackers exploit the use of the buffer space that they use this attack. The small in-process queue if the target system will be flooded with connection requests from the device of the attackers. However, when the target system replies to those requests, it doesn't respond. And while waiting for the response from the device of the attacker, the process will cause the target system to time out. Ultimately, when the connection queue fills up, it makes the system to become unusable or crash. For you to countermeasure a TCPSYN flood attacks, here are some preventions:

- On open connections, decrease the timeout, and increase the size of the connection queue
- For you to stop inbound SYN packets, place servers behind a firewall configured

Chapter 4: Types of Malware

The unwanted software that someone installs in your system without your consent is the precise definition of malicious software. There can be a legitimate attachment of this software to propagate and code, meaning that, across the Internet, it can replicate itself or lurk useful applications. A few common malware types include:

Spyware

They use spyware to collect user's browsing habits, their computer, as well as their information. And without your knowledge, spyware tracks everything you do, and a remote user gets those data. Also, spyware can have malicious programs from the Internet installed or downloaded. When you install another freeware application, spyware is usually a separate program that is installed unknowingly and its working is quite similar to adware.

Adware

Companies use adware, a software application for marketing purposes. When any program is running, there will be a display of the advertising banners. While you browse any website, you can download adware automatically to your computer. On the screen of your computer, through a bar or pop-up, you can view it.

Ransomware

This type of malware threatens to delete or publish the data of the victim after blocking them unless there will be payment of a ransom by the victim. The more advanced malware utilizes the cryptoviral extortion technique. Doing this will encrypt the files of the victim and without the decryption key, makes it almost impossible to recover. It can be quite hard for a knowledgeable individual to reverse the lock on the system with the use of some simple computer ransomware.

Droppers

For the installation of viruses on computers, they make use of a program called a dropper. Virus-scanning software cannot detect a dropper since it is not affected by malicious code in several instances. Also, for virus software that is resident on a compromised system, a dropper can connect to the internet and download updates.

Worms

Worms propagate across computers and networks as self-contained programs, and since they have no attachment to a host file, they differ from viruses. They use email attachment to spread worms and it gets activated when you open the program. Apart from conducting malicious activities, the worm can also send a copy of itself to all contact of the email address of an infected computer. Then, there can be an event of denial-of-service attacks against nodes on the network when a worm spreads across the internet and overload email servers.

Logic Bombs

Appended to an application is a type of malicious software, which is a logic bomb. A specific occurrence triggers it such as a specific time and date or a logical condition.

Trojans

Usually, Trojans has a malicious function and are hidden in a useful program. Since Trojans do not replicate, this major trait separates it from viruses. Also, attackers can exploit a backdoor established by a Trojan to launch attacks on a system. For example, so hackers can perform an attack after using it to listen, they can program a Trojan to open a high-numbered port.

Stealth Viruses

For stealth viruses to conceal themselves, they take over the functions of a system. The report of the software is that of uninfected since they have compromised the malware detection. They change the time and date of the last modification of the file and conceal any increase in the size of an infected file.

Polymorphic Viruses

When the viruses vary cycles of decryption and encryption, they use this process to conceal themselves. So, initially decrypted by a decryption program is a connected mutation engine and the encrypted virus. A code area will be thus be infected by the encrypted virus. Then, there will be a development of a new decryption routine by the mutation engine. Using an algorithm corresponding to the new decryption routine, a copy of the virus and the mutation engine will then be encrypted by the virus. The new code will then have an attachment of the encrypted package of virus and mutation engine. Thus, the process continues to repeat itself. It is quite tricky to detect such viruses. However, due to the several modifications of their source code, they have a high level of entropy. For quick detection, you can use Process Hacker.

System or Boot-Record Infections

The hard disks will give a record of a boot-record by the virus attached to the master boot. So it can propagate to other computers and disks, it will look at the boot sector and load the virus into memory when you start the system.

File Infectors

These types of viruses associate themselves with executable code like .exe files. As the code loads, the virus will be installed. And with the creation of a virus file with a similar name, which is an .exe extension, another version of a file infector will connect itself with a file. Thus, the virus code will execute when the file is opened.

Macro Viruses

Those that get infected by these viruses are applications like Excel or Microsoft Word. Macro viruses attach to the initialization sequence of an application. Before it transfers control to the application, the virus executes instructions when the application is opened. In the computer system, there will be a replication of the virus before it attaches to other codes.

Chapter 5: How the Hacking Process Works

System information leakage is the primary use of hacking before. There is now dark connotation connected to hack in the recent years, courtesy of some villain players. On the other hand, for them to be assured of their systems' weaknesses and strengths, hackers are employed by various corporations to do this. They earn a fat salary through a positive trust they build, and also, they are aware of the point that they need to stop. So, without further ado, let's make a deep dive into the art of hacking.

Preparation Phase

A programming language is highly required here. Though you will see some essential guidelines, you must not restrict yourself to a specific language. Tolerance is quite needed in this stage because it might take time to learn programming language.

- It is compulsory to know assembly language. Though there are several variables of it, your processor understands only this language. Also, when you don't know assembly, exploiting a program may not be possible.
- You will also need to know bash scripting. The manipulation of Linux/Unix systems will be done with ease, including getting most of the job done for you through writing scripts.
- Since PHP is what most web applications use, you must try to learn PHP, and also, in this field, a reasonable choice for you is perl.
- You can also automate several tasks with powerful, high-level scripting languages like Ruby and Python.
- The languages they used in building Windows and Linux are C++ and C. most especially; it teaches how memory works and also assemble language.

Then, your target needs to be in the picture. This process is referred to as enumeration, which is how you will gather vital information about your target. You will have fewer surprises when you know more about your target in advance.

Now, the process of hacking can begin. For your commands,

put a *nix terminal into use. For users of Windows, a *nix will help in emulation through Cygwin. Nmap doesn't need Cygwin as it runs on Windows and uses WinPCap. However, because of the lack of raw sockets, Nmap doesn't work well on Windows systems. Also, because of their flexibility, BSD and Linux must be in your list of considerations. And there are several pre-installed tools with several Linux distributions. Alternatively, in the Windows Store, you can find a *nix terminal on Windows 10 fall Creators Updates or later and courtesy of Windows Linux Subsystem, the Linux command-line can be emulated by Windows.

Now, the first step is to secure your system. For you to give enough protection to yourself, you need to quite understand all common techniques. You need an authorization from your target for you to attack as you begin with the fundamentals. You can do this by using virtual machines to set up your laboratory, ask for written permission from your target, or even attack your network. You will get in trouble if you attempt to attack a network because it is illegal, no matter its content.

The process of testing your target is the next stage. Will you be able to get to the remote system? Though it is what most operating systems use, the result of using the ping utility to be sure your target is alive may not be quite concrete. Paranoid administrators of systems can easily shut it off since it relies on the ICMP protocol. Then, you will need to define the OS. When you intend to run a port scan, try nmap or pOf. So you can make your plan of action; running a scan of the ports will tell you the kind of router or firewall your target is using and you will see the ports that are open on the OS and the machine. Then, you can use the -o switch to activate OS detection in nmap.

By now, you would have discovered an open port or a path in the system. Most times, there is a strong protection for certain ports like HTTP (80) and FTP (20).

- The evidence of a secure shell, SSH, service running on the target is an open port 22, and this can be brute force sometimes.
- It is possible your target could have forgotten other UDP and TCP ports, including several UDP ports left open for LAN gaming and also Telnet.

The next process is the authentication after you must have cracked the password. Brute force is among several techniques you can use to crack a password. You can try every potential password that a predefined dictionary of brute force software contains.

- Most times, finding your way into a system tends to be much easier even without cracking the password
- For you to upload it to the secure site, you can go for a TCP scan installation or acquire a rooted tablet. Then, you will cause the password to appear on your proxy when the IP address opens
- It may not be a good idea to attempt a login to a remote machine using every possible password. While it may take some time to complete, it could pollute the system

logs, and intrusion detection systems can detect it easily

- For you to crack password quickly, you may result in using Rainbow Tables. You need to understand that it is only if the hash of the password is in your possession can the password cracking be a good method
- As it is thousands of times faster, another processor is the newer techniques that use the graphics card
- You can get a massive speed boost by cutting the MD5 algorithms and also exploiting the weaknesses of most hashing algorithms can significantly improve the speed of the cracking since they are generally weak
- Brute force can take a lot of time since users are using strong passwords. However, brute force techniques have improved with several major improvements

The privilege of a super-user is what you need to get now. If it is a Windows system you are trying to crack, you will need administrator privileges, and if your target is a *nix machine, the root privileges are all you need.

- You may not be able to access all the features of a connection that you gain access into. However, you can do everything if you have the root, administrator, or super-user account
- Except it has been altered, the admin account comes by default for routers, and it is administrator account for Windows
- You may require a specific level of authentication for you to get the most information because they have all been protected. You will require super-user privileges to see all the files on a computer. In BSD and Linux OS, root users get similar privileges as a user account

Now, you may want to engage in some different tricks. Most

times, you may want to bump up your authorization level by causing the memory to dump so you can inject code or perform a task at a higher level by creating a buffer overflow to gain super-user status.

- You can do this by finding or writing an insecure program that you can execute on their machine
- If the bugged software has setuid bit set, this will happen in Unix-like systems, and as such, it is as a super-user that the program will be executed

You may want to have a backdoor developed at this stage. It tends to be ideal that you can come back again when you have gained complete access to a system. You can backdoor certain essential system services like the SSH server. Though, during the next upgrade of the system, your backdoor may be removed. Then, the solution is to backdoor also the compiler itself so you have a possible way of coming back through every compiled software. And your tracks must be covered. It is quite critical that the system administrator knows nothing about the compromise of the system. Never have more than necessary files created or make a change to the website. Also, you don't need to create more users. Make fast actions. Ensure that your secret password is hard-coded anytime you patch a server like SSHD. Though without containing any crucial information, the server must let them in if anyone attempts to login with this password.

Chapter 6: Why Hackers Use Linux

There are several special features on the Linux operating system that make it more dominating than any other OS. With Unix as its old version, the operating system of Linux is an open source. Day by day, there is a rapid development in the use of Linux. And rather than using any other operating systems such as Mac or Windows, hackers like to use Linux because of the additional benefits Linux operating system has over others. The operating system of Linux has remarkable special features that make it more dominating than other systems even though their operating systems are more user-friendly.

Why Hackers Prefer Linux Operating System

For the challenge of it, and because they want to make money from their natural hacking capacities, hackers break into the networks of computers or standalone personal computer systems. And to test their skills, hackers will need the operating system, which offers maximum security. Thus, Linux appears to be the best choice for hackers since it makes it more secure for them in all of their activities. For libraries and Linux applications, they have written millions of lines of code today. This process has allowed it to be integrated into broadly diverse projects as it is done in an extremely modular manner. For example, you can have a part of a library used as a network hijacking code, even with it allowing you to sniff the network for proactive performance monitoring. Also, network security can be hacked with ease.

As it is flexible, hackers have the opportunity of playing their entire fashionable activities using the playground of Linux. Also, it is quite simple for hackers to understand, learn, and use Linux since they can use their penetrating testing methods to know if there is insecurity. Linux is quite secure since when problems arise, hackers can patch it because they have the ability to look at each and every line of Linux code. It can also be used at any time by any user working on it and not only some programmers working in some corporate organizations. Here are some of the benefits of Linux over others:

Easy to Use

The general belief is that Linux is only for hackers and

programmers, and that tends to be the widespread myth. However, this analog is far from being the truth. You will easily have a basic understanding of Linux if you have been using it for some time. It is not the same as the operating system of Windows. As such, it could be quite tricky when we make the switch to a different operating system. You will find Linux to be user-friendly and more convenient than Windows.

Less RAM Consumption

Linux consumes lesser processing utility and RAM as well as requires lesser space for disk since it is quite light. Thus, you can have other operating systems such as Windows and OS X installed with it.

Linux is the Future

First, Android is based on Linux and also, the choice for web servers is the Linux operating system for its robustness, flexibility, and stability.

No Requirement for Drivers

You don't need separate drivers before you can use Linux. Within the Linux kernel, you will find all the necessary drivers you will need when you install Linux. As a result, to install drivers for hardware, you won't need CDs anymore.

Serious Take on Privacy

All over the Internet, many people are talking about Windows 10 and the issue of privacy. Usually, your data is collected by Windows 10. However, there is no case of anyone collecting information and data about you for monetary gain when you use Linux operating system.

Hacking Tools are Often Written for Linux

Nmap and Metasploit, some of the popular hacking tools are ported for Windows. However, Linux has some better tools and in a much better way, manages memory, and not all capabilities are transferred from Linux.

Several Programming Languages Have the Support of Linux

Most programming languages have abundant support from Linux. On Linux, working perfectly are Perl, Python, Ruby, PHP, Java, and C++/C. It is effective and simple when you want to use Linux for any of the scripting languages.

Less Vulnerable

There is so much vulnerability in virtually all the operating systems available except Linux. Linux has fewer vulnerabilities, and it prides itself as the most secure operating system.

Low Cost

It is widely known that Linux is an open-source operating system and so, you can get it online for free as well as freely install and use app the applications without any payment.

Flexibility

You can use Linux for high-performance desktop and server applications, as well as embedded systems.

Maintenance

It is quite easy to maintain the operating system of Linux. You can install all the software with ease. It is even easier to search for their software since every variant of Linux has its central software repository.

Portable and Light

From nearly any Linux distribution that they want, the customized live boot drives and disks are there for hackers to develop. Since the resources it consumes are quite fewer, it is quick to install. The fact that it consumes fewer resources makes Linux light-weight.

Command-Line Interface

Windows and Mac don't have the specially designed, highly-integrated, and strong command-line interface which Linux boasts of having. Other Linux users and hackers will have control over their system with greater access.

Multitasking

All at the same time, you can make use of Linux, as that is how it is designed. For example, your other works will not experience any form of slowdown with a large printing job in the background. Also, your primary processes will not be disturbed even with several works done at the same time.

Network Friendly

Linux is effective in managing network over it since it offers several commands and libraries that hackers use to test network penetrations. Hence, as an open-source operating system, the team that contributes to it does so over the internet network. Also, more than any other operating system, Linux makes network backup faster as a reliable operating system.

Stability

When you want to maintain performance levels, the only OS that doesn't require any periodic rebooting is Linux. Also, the cause of memory leaks cannot slow it down or make it freeze up too. For many years, you can continue to use this operating system.

Since hackers can increase their hacking capabilities and also test their skills on this operating system, it makes Linux as their best choice. The setup programs and installation is user-friendly, and several Linux distributions have tools that make installation of more software quite user-friendly.

Chapter 7: Kali Linux Installation and Updates

A security-focused operating system is one of the most essential things to have when you are looking for a career in information security. You can efficiently perform tedious and time-consuming tasks with the help of a suitable operating system. At present, the operating systems of Linux are indeed countless. However, one of the best choices is Kali Linux. cybersecurity professionals use it for assessing network security, ethical hacking, and penetration testing.

Kali Linux will be one of the first names to be mentioned when it comes to offensive Linux distributions, hacking, and penetration testing. There are several information security tasks as various command-line hacking tools that Linux comes pre-packaged like application security, computer forensics, network security, and penetration testing. Fundamentally, when you attempt to engage in ethical hacking, the operating system of Linux is an ultimate solution.

Kali Linux Installation

The process of installing Kali Linux can be quite simple, and the options of installation are numerous. The techniques most people prefer are:

1. Using the operating system to dual boot Kali Linux
2. With virtualization software like VirtualBox or VMware
3. Installation of hard disk for Kali Linux
4. Making a Kali Linux bootable USB drive while installing Kali Linux

The focus will be on using virtualization software to install Kali Linux even while there are several options available. For you to perform a comprehensive penetration test using all the tools you need, you can set up your machine by following these steps.

Requirements for Installation

- USB support / DVD-CD drive
- While working with VirtualBox or VMware, the recommendation is around 4 GB
- The recommendation for your hard drive is a minimum free space of 20 GB

The Installation Process

Step 1: VMware installation:

First, a kind of virtualization software is essential to run Kali Linux. For many people, there is a preference for VMware even when they can use VirtualBox by Oracle as part of several options that they can choose from. From your applications folder, launch VMware when you have finished with the installation.

Step 2: Kali Linux download and image integrity checking:

You can choose the one that best suits your needs when you go to the official download page to download Kali Linux. Also, there are some hexadecimal numbers on the download page. There is nothing so important about them. Also, for the tasks that are related to security is the intention of Kali Linux. As such, the integrity checking of your downloaded image is highly required. The file's SHA-256 fingerprint needs to be checked and make a comparison with the one you see on the site you make the download.

Step 3: a new virtual machine launch:

You will hit the 'create a new virtual machine' button when you get to the homepage of the VMware Workstation Pro. Before you configure the details of virtual machine, you must have chosen the guest operating system after selecting the iso file of Kali Linux. Choose the Kali Linux VM to start the virtual machine, and you will click on the green button with 'power on' inscription. You will see the machine starting up!

The process of installation

In the GRUB menu, you will get the prompt to choose your preferred mode of installation when the machine is powered up. Before you continue, choose the graphical installation. You will be taken to another page where you will be prompted to choose your layout for the keyboard, the location of your country, and the language you prefer. Then, the loader will have the related settings of your network configured after installing extra components when you are through with the local information. Then, for this installation, a domain and hostname will be prompted by the installer. Before you continue with the installation, you will have to provide the appropriate information for the environment. You will press continue when you have set a password for the Kali Linux machine. An important note here: make sure you keep your password carefully! Then, set your time zone will be prompted by the installer after you must have set your password. At the partitioning of the disk, it will pause. From the disk partition, four choices will be provided to you by the installer. The 'guided – use entire disk' option is the easiest of them all. For additional granular configuration options, the method of 'manual' partitioning can only be used by experienced users. If you are a new user, the recommendation is to choose all files when you are choosing the partitioning disk and you can click on 'continue.' Then, on the host machine, the entire changes you want to make can then be confirmed. You must be careful here since you can have the data on the disk erased if you continue.

So, the process of file installation will be run through by the installer when you confirm the changes in the partition. As this process can take some minutes, the installation will be done automatically. If you prefer to obtain future pieces of updates and software, the setup for a network mirror will be inquired by the system when the necessary files are installed. If you want to use the repositories of Kali, make sure you have this functionality enabled. Then, the related files of the package manager will be configured. Next, the boot loader of GRUB is the next thing you will be asked to install. Choose 'yes,' and since it will be required to boot Kali, you will choose the device to write the important information for boot loader to the hard drive. To finish the installation, hit the 'continue' button when the installation of GRUB to the disk has finished. Then, specific files for the final stage will be installed. By now, brace up yourself because your journey of exploring Kali Linux has just begun since you have successfully installed Kali.

Updating Kali Linux

The packages index list is the first step of an update for your Kali Linux system. You will enter the following command when you open the terminal;

```
$ sudo apt update
```

As an option, for all scheduled packages for update, you can display them. You have the opportunity of upgrading all packages at once with the use of `apt install PACKAGE-NAME` as well as individual package upgrade at this stage. Now, you have completely upgraded your Kali Linux.

Chapter 8: Installing Kali Linux on Virtual Machine

In similar hardware that you currently have, you can run different operating systems in a number of ways. And some of the options available for you are hard disks, USBs, and DVDs. In this chapter, the assumption is that for you to run your Kali Linux, you have no dedicated computer and as such, we are going to use a virtual PC or a virtualized environment to run it. You must have had virtual box installed on your computer for us to begin the process. And in case you don't have it on your system, it is free to download when you go to the official website of VirtualBox. For the hardware that we will be using to install Kali Linux, this software will be emulating this hardware.

It is widely known that unless you have access to software, it can be quite tricky to download such software. Thus, you will download Kali Linux ISO image from its official page. And in case you want to follow along as you mirror that, the flavor of the Kali Linux KDE 64-bit is what we will be using. The size of its download is around 3.2 GB, and for you to download, it might take a while. You will then have the .ISO image mounted into the virtual machine when you have dealt with that one. If you have the intention of using it in another machine, you can have it burned into a USB or bootable DVD. However, you may need to take into account certain considerations. Then, you may open VirtualBox when the image is downloaded.

Now, you will hit on the 'new' button for you to create a new virtual machine, which is the first thing you will do. Then, in the natural operational system, you will have to specify the existence of this machine's files of the service files. You can select Linux for type because it is on top Linux that Kali is built. And for version, Ubuntu 64-bit will be your choice. Though to get Kali up and running on VirtualBox, it is an ideal default setting for us. There is no guarantee it will work perfectly by specifying version and type. Then, the prompt for the amount of memory we want will be the next. You can go for 2GB as even 1GB will still work. Alternatively, you can go ahead and give it as much as you want if you have enough memory.

The hard drive setup is the next step here, which the VirtualBox will ask you. You may choose to use an existing one or create one. So as not to go back and forth between several emulators, you can select VirtualBox Disk Image after selecting the hard drive file type. If you are using VMware, for instance, a more suitable option will be VHD. After that, your storage allocation on the physical hard drive is the next option to choose. Then, you can select dynamic allocation. Next, the amount of allocation for this machine is what you will now choose. You must consider checking how much memory you have available before you go ahead with this action. The place you want to keep your virtual disks can be specified inside VirtualBox. You may then go ahead and hit the 'create' button. But, that is not the end of the process. For us to be sure we can understand them, we may want to play around the main settings. For future reference, you will have the freedom of tackling the virtual environment and this is quite essential. You may want to read more on the topic of virtual machine settings because it is an extensive topic.

You can as well move on to the system settings since, during the creation process, you have covered some items. If you don't have a floppy drive, you can remove floppy under the system. You can prompt VirtualBox to check for any media in the DVD player first in the boot order. It is useful to know that in the initial install, that is the base for our Kali image. If it is necessary, you may want to check that later also, but you can have 2MB for the base memory. As per the above image, ensure that you mirror the extended features. Then, you can boost the memory of the image up to around 128 MB when you move on to 'Display.' Also, in case you want to get naughty with specific graphics, you can have the 3D acceleration enabled. You may run the risk of burning some circuitry and do not give it excessive video memory of you are running on old hardware. After that, you can do one of the most vital settings, which is to check the storage. Ensure that the image file you have downloaded from the official page of Kali Linux is pointing to the empty CD-ROM drive. Also, for you to be given the options to choose your .ISO file, you can achieve that by clicking on the disc icon under attributes.

Now, it is believed that you have mounted the CD-ROM image since the drive represents the .ISO image. You can leave the live DVD/CD checkbox as default and not tick it. You will have to pay attention to the main configuration by checking the settings for the network. Some of them are:

- Generic networking
- Host-only networking
- Internal networking
- Bridged networking
- NAT networking
- Network Address Translation, NAT
- Not attached

You can go to the official page of VirtualBox for you to know more about each mode. And provided your internet connection is wired, this default mode could be enough if all you want to do is to view email inside the guest, download files, and browse the web. As it is for the beginners, you can, for now, use NAT. When you launch the machine, everything should be working well if you are connected via an Ethernet cable. Without an interface card, it may not be possible for you to reach the web in case you don't have a wired connection. Then, you only have to hit on the 'start' to launch the operating system if you intend running Kali in a virtual environment.

Chapter 9: How to Organize Kali Linux

 Kali 2.0 was launched by Offensive Security after ten years of evolution. And of all the Kali/Backtrack releases, the easiest to use by far is Kali 2.0. There are some new features with the new Kali if you are used to the original Kali. However, there's nothing better than this! They have streamlined and reorganized the menus completely with a helpful icon representing many of the tools. Here are some new things about Kali 2.0:

- Built-in screencasting
- Desktop notifications
- For faster Metasploit loading, there is a native Ruby 2.0
- New categories and menus
- New user interface

They have streamlined the Kali 2.0 quite well, and compared to earlier versions of Backtrack/Kali; the layout flows quite well. As it is laid out in a concise and clear manner, the feel is that of having everything at your fingertips. To organize your Kali, you can follow the following ways as we examine some of its components.

Overview of the Desktop

Again, everything you will need is at your fingertips on the desktop, which feels and looks quite good.

Apache Webserver

At present, it seems they have removed the Apache web server for restart, start, and stop service icons from Kali 2.0. Well, you may want to use the command below if you want to start them from a terminal prompt:

- To restart – you can use "`/etc/init.d/apache2 restart`' or "service apache2 restart"
- To stop – you can use "`/etc/init.d/apache2 stop`" or "service apache2 stop"
- To start – you can use "`/etc/init.d/apache2 start`" or "service apache2 start"

You will notice the change from Kali 1 concerning the default webpage as you can now surf the webserver of Kali. Now, located in a folder called HTTP, there is one level deeper for the root website as well. As such, instead of the old directory "/var/www/," you can now drop the folders or pages of your website into the directory "/var/www/html/" when you use the Apache server.

Screencasting

You can now use screencasting because there is a built-in screencasting feature in Kali 2.0. You have the ability to record in real-time the adventures of your security testing.

Places Menu

Within your Kali, you have links to various locations contained in the Places menu.

Workspaces

There are also workspaces in the earlier versions of Backtrack/Linux. Workspace is the additional desktop screens that you can use in case you don't know the workspace. For all the windows that you have opened, you can get an overview of them using the 'super key.' Also, you can open the workspace menu if you have a touch-screen monitor. Between the workspaces, you will have the ability of dragging and dropping specific running programs.

Auto-Minimizing Windows

At times, some windows disappear or auto-minimize, which is another thing in the new Kali 2.0. On the favorite bar, to the left of the associated icon, you will see a white circle when a window is minimized. The first terminal window will appear if you click on the terminal icon once, and both minimized terminal windows will reappear when you click it twice. Also, to see minimized windows, you can press "Alt-tab." Then, to see additional windows, you can arrow around when you have the "alt-tab" pressed.

Command-Line Tools

It is in the directory "/usr/share that they have the majority of tools installed. When you type the names of these tools in a terminal, you can run these tools and also other tools in the menu. For you to familiarize yourself with both the share directory and the menu system, you may want to take a few moments on that.

Application Menu

Under the Application menu, you will see the location of a list of common program favorites. And by type, there is a logical layout of the tools. For example, if you want to see the most common web app testing tools, all you have to do is click on the Web Application Analysis menu item. You will see a list of all of the tools for a specific category. It is due to the fact the top tools are shown by the menu system, and in Kali, not all of the tools are available. Essentially, available in the menu system of Kali are only a fraction of the installed tools and it is only from the command-line that most of the tools can be available.

Favorites Bar

On the desktop's left side, you will see a customizable "Favorite bar" in the new Kali. With this, you can get into the action quickly since you can get the applications you use most time with this menu list. Through the required dependencies, you can start the represented tool automatically with just a click. For example, before you launch Metasploit, if you want to be sure you have created the default database, you can prestart the database software by clicking on the button for Metasploit. Then, you can see various applications on the bottom of the favorites bar by clicking on the "show applications." In folders, you can arrange the programs by type. You can also use the search bar by typing what you want if you don't see the app you are looking for.

Chapter 10: Scanning (nmap, massscan, hping3) and Managing Networks (Wireshark)

During the course of penetration testing, a very essential host detector and network scanning tool are network mapped, nmap. Mainly, they use nmap as a security scanner and vulnerability detector which makes it a powerful utility as well as using it to enumerate and gather information. Since it can run on several different operating systems such as Mac, BSD, Linux, and Windows, this makes nmap a multipurpose tool. They use nmap for several powerful purposes including:

- Securing holes and detecting the vulnerability, such as nmap scripts
- Operating system detection, software version, and hardware address

- It works for service discovery, that is, detecting the version and software to the respective port
- Port enumeration and discovery; detecting ports that are open on the host
- Host discovery; detecting the live host on the network

As a common tool, nmap is available for both the graphical user interface and command-line interface. And to perform scanning, nmap utilizes several methods, some of which are FTP bounce scanning, TCP reverse ident scanning, TCP connect() scanning, and many more.

Effective Use of nmap

Since we have a difference between an advance scanning and basic, simple scanning, the target machine has a huge dependence on the usage of nmap. For us to get the right outcome by bypassing the intrusion preventive/detection software and firewall, there is a need to make use of advanced techniques. You will see some examples below of a few basic commands their usage:

On the target system, if you intend to scan a specific port, such as scanning only on the target computer Telnet, FTP, and HTTP, then you will need relevant parameter to use the nmap command. Also, you may as well call the file in the exclude parameter if the lists of IP addresses that you intend to exclude are contained in a file that you have. Another scenario is that since it tends to be dangerous for you, you may want to exclude specific IP addresses if you want to scan the entire subnet. As such, use the excluding parameter when you use the nmap command. You will need to add an -sL parameter to the command if you intend to see the entire list of the hosts that you are scanning.

Enumerating a Huge Quantity of Hosts with Massscan

For a while now, massscan has been around, and all around the world, pentesters are making use of it. In a second, masscan can transmit up to 10 million packets as a reconnaissance tool. Massscan utilizes a custom IP/TCP stack and asynchronous transmission with different reception and transmission of packets using different threads.

You can quickly enumerate a vast amount of hosts using massscan. Essentially, massscan can scan the whole internet as quickly as 6 minutes, according to the author of the tool. And because of the high rate of its transmission, they also use massscan for stress testing. For anyone to accomplish those high rates, they will need special drivers like NICs and PF_RING. Since it interacts with the use of similar style of nmap, this part makes it a convenient tool.

Massscan Features

- Custom IP/TCP stack
- Basic vulnerability scanning such as heartbleed
- Banner grabbing
- Nmap style target option and specification
- Nmap style output
- Ultrafast port scanning: up to 10M packets per second in transmission (requiring PF_RING drivers and capable – NIC)

Uses of Masscan

- Random scanning for knowledge or fun
- Internet enumeration
- Enumeration of several subnets within an organization
- Enumeration of a large number of hosts
- For the mapping of the network, massscan can be used as the first recon tool

Hping3 as a Packet Generator and Network Scanning Tool

As a free analyzer and packet generator for the IP/TCP protocol for the Antirez distribution, hping is a network scanning tool. For network security, hping3 is one kind of a tester, and for security testing and auditing of networks and firewalls, it is one of the de facto tools. They also use it for the exploitation of the idle scan scanning method, which now has its implementation in the nmap security scanner. As an analyzer/assembler for IP/TCP packet, a command-line oriented is the network scanning tool hping. Even when hping can do more than sending ICMP echo requests, the ping(8) Unix command inspired the interface. Its features include the ability to send files between a covered channel, possession of a traceroute mode, and support for RAW-IP, ICMP, UDP, and TCP protocols. In the past, they only used hping as a network scanning tool. However, some people use it in several manners to test hosts and networks.

Some of the Usages of hping Network Scanning Tool

- Network scanning tool
- Using Tk interface, it is simple to use networking utilities
- Prototype IDS systems
- Security and networking research in the event of emulating complicated IP/TCP behaviour
- Concept exploits proof
- Automated firewalling tests
- Write real applications related to IP/TCP security and testing
- Learn IP/TCP
- Networking research
- Exploitation of identified vulnerabilities of IP/TCP stacks
- Test IDSes

- Test firewalling rules
- Perform the idle scan (with an easy user interface for implementation in nmap)
- Using the standard utilities network scanning tool to probe/ping/traceroute hosts behind a firewall that blocks attempts
- Students learning IP/TCP can also get adequate knowledge through hping
- Auditing IP/TCP stacks
- Remote uptime guessing
- Remote OS fingerprinting
- Advanced traceroute, under all the supported protocols
- Manual path MTU discovery
- Using fragmentation, TOS, and different protocols for network testing
- Advanced port scanning
- Firewall testing

Securing and Monitoring Your Network with Wireshark

The toolkit for a network security analyst is one of the most powerful tools known as wireshark that people also referred to before as Ethereal. Through a variety of levels, from bits comprising a single packet to information on connection, wireshark can examine the details of traffic as it peers inside the network as a network packet analyzer. Wireshark can troubleshoot security issues in the network of a device and also analyze security events through its depth and flexibility inspection. Since it is free, the price of wireshark is also great!

Wireshark Installation

It is as simple as ABC to install wireshark. For Mac OS X or Windows, you can download the binary versions. Also, for most flavors of Unix/Linux, there's availability of wireshark through the standard software distribution systems. And on other operating systems, the source code is available for installation. For the Windows version, the team that developed wireshark built it on top of the WinPcap packet capture library. And if you don't have WinPcap already in your installation and you are using Windows, you may have to have it installed to run it. Here is a caveat: before you run wireshark installer, you can use the manual process to remove an outdated version of WinPcap through the "Add/Remove Programs" in the control panel. The process of installation is the same with the wizard-based sequence that uses two main prompts: at startup, it will ask if you intend to start the WinPcap Netgroup Packet Filter, NPF service and if you want to have WinPcap installed. For you to capture packets, you can choose the former option that will allow you even if you don't have administrator privileges. It is only administrators that will be able to run wireshark if you have this service enabled.

Chapter 11: Firewalls

Based on a set of security rules, when you intend to block or permit data packets as well as monitor outgoing and incoming network traffic, a network security device that you can use is a firewall. For a firewall to block malicious traffic such as hackers and viruses, you will need to establish a barrier between your incoming traffic and internal network from external sources. You can improve the connection of computer security like the internet or LAN when you use tools like firewalls. An integral part of your network's comprehensive security framework is the firewall. With the use of a code wall that inspects each individual data packet as it arrives, the firewall's either side, both outbound and inbound from the system, to determine whether it can give it access to be blocked or pass, a firewall completely isolates your computer from the Internet.

When it enables granular control over the kinds of system processes and functions that have access to the resources of networking, you can further enhance the security through the capability of firewalls. For it to deny or allow traffic, there are several host conditions and signatures that these firewalls use. You can operate, setup, and install firewalls relatively easily even when they sound complex. The belief of some people is that when they have a firewall installed, the traffic that passes through the network segment will be controlled. However, a firewall that is host-based can be suitable for you. On your computer, you can have them executed, including using it with Internet Connection Firewall, ICF. Fundamentally, there is a similarity to the function of the two firewalls; to stop intrusion and offer a strong technique of access control policy. To put it simply, as access control policy enforcement points, a firewall is a system that safeguards your computer.

Functions of Firewalls

In essence, here are some of the basic functions of firewalls:

- Act as an intermediary
- Report and record events
- Control and manage network traffic
- Validate access
- Defend resources

The Definition of Personal Firewall

In the world of secure computing, it's quite essential for you to understand your need for a firewall. And since it aids our understanding of how a firewall may address those needs, we need to understand the goals of information security.

The Need for Personal Firewall

Electronically, you will connect your computer to a broad network in the times of high-speed Internet access. You will have limited protection or control unless you have installed a personal firewall. There are some drawbacks to any high-speed connection, typical of anything else. Ironically, the same feature that makes a connection with a high-speed vulnerable is the same reason that makes it attractive. In some ways, you may be leaving your front door of your house unlocked and open with your connection to the high-speed internet. Some of the features of high-speed internet connections include:

- Constant active connection – this is the fact that when your computer is connected to the internet every time, it is vulnerable
- Access of high-speed – this means that it can be quite faster for intruders to break into your computer

- A regular IP – it will be easier for an intruder to find your computer again and again after they have discovered you

Using a Personal Firewall for Defense

Compared to an ordinary 56Kbps connection, now it is clear to you how, when you are online on a high-speed internet connection, you are vulnerable. Now, the threat posed by this type of connection is now known to you, and how you can defend yourself against it is what you need to know. Here are some of the vital reasons for a personal firewall:

- You can easily develop policies for security to suit your individual needs since most personal firewalls are highly configurable
- When your computer's program tries to connect to the internet, you wish to be kept informed
- The home network that you run requires you to keep it isolated from the internet
- You use a public WiFi network when you connect to the internet in an airport, café, or park
- With an 'always on' broadband connection, you surf the internet at home

Firewalls Types

Though the two are suitable, you can have firewalls as hardware or software. With port applications and numbers, you can regulate traffic through the installation of a software firewall program on your computer while you can install the hardware firewall type between the gateway and your network. The most common firewall type is the packet-filtering firewalls, and in case they don't match an established security rule set, they prevent packets from passing through after they have examined them. The purpose of these firewall types is to analyze the destination and source of the packets for IP addresses. It will thus be trusted to enter the network if the packets match those of an 'allowed' rule on the firewall.

Stateless and stateful are the two categories of the packet-filtering firewalls. The ones that are easy targets for hackers are the stateless firewalls since they lack context by examining packets independently of one another. On the other hand, stateful firewalls tend to be much more secure because they remember information about previously passed packets. Though packet-filtering firewalls ultimately offer quite basic protection and tend to be quite inadequate, they can be indeed effective. For example, for them to determine the adverse effect of the application that the content of the requests is reaching can be quite hard for them. Thus, there will be no way for the firewall to know when there could be a deletion of a database from a misconceived trusted source if it allows a malicious request. Those that are equipped to detect such threats are the proxy and next-generation firewalls.

SMLI, Stateful Multilayer Inspection Firewalls

While these firewalls compare them against trusted packets, they filter packets at the application, transport, and network layers. Also, if they pass the layer individually, SMLI only allows them to pass after they examined the entire packet, which is typical of NGFW firewalls. They ensure the potential of all initiated communications happening only with trusted sources as they determine the state of the communication and also by examining the packets.

NAT, Network Address Translation Firewalls

These firewalls keep individual IP address hidden when they use a single IP address to connect to the internet by allowing several devices with independent network addresses. As such, they offer greater security against attacks because attackers can't capture specific details when they are scanning a network for IP addresses. These firewalls are rooted between outside traffic and a group of computers with proxy firewalls having similarities with NAT firewalls.

Proxy Firewalls

At the level of application, these firewalls have the network filtered. They are planted between two end systems, which are not like the basic firewalls. The firewall must receive a request from the client and using a set of security for the evaluation, and after that, keep it blocked or give permission. Essentially, layer 7 protocols like FTP and HTTP are monitored by proxy firewalls and for them to detect malicious traffic, they utilize both deep packet and stateful inspections.

NGFW, Next-Generation Firewalls

These firewalls blend additional functionality with the technology of traditional firewall like anti-virus, intrusion prevention systems, encrypted traffic inspection, and many more. Essentially, it has the inclusion of DPI, deep packet inspection. It is within the packet itself that deep packet inspection examines the data while looking at packet headers is what basic firewalls only look. With this process, users can stop, categorize, and identify packets effectively with malicious data.

Chapter 12: Obtaining User Information: Maltego, Scraping, Shodan/Censys.io

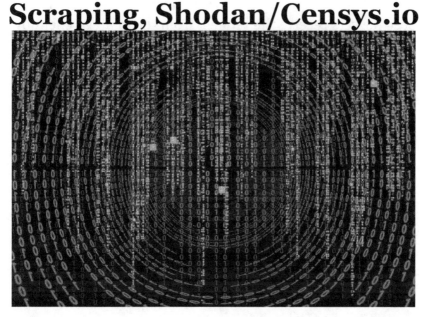

Maltego reveals how information is connected to each other as a forensic and open-source application. The relationship between several information types can aid in identifying the unknown relationship as well as giving a better picture of their links. When you use maltego, you will have the ability to find relationships and also the people's link, such as mutual friends, social profiles, websites, and companies with the gathered information relationships. You may want to gather the connection between net blocks, DNS names, and domains if you intend to gather information regarding any infrastructure.

Architecture of Maltego

Seed servers receive the request from the maltego client over HTTPS in XML format. Then, it is the TAS servers that will take the request from the seed server before the service provider then get the request. The maltego client will then get the results of the request. For more privacy, you may want to consider having your TAS servers. At present, the basic and professional modules are the two types of maltego, and the availability of the modules are the two major differences between both servers. CTAS is what the basic server has while in the professional server, you will see the PTTAS, SQLTAS, and CTAS.

From within maltego, you can perform several pentesting related tasks with PTTAS, including banner grabbing, port scan, and so on. Also, accessing SQL database is possible for TAS through SQLTAS. You can also get results after performing numerous SQL queries using this module. Postgress, Oracle, DB2, MSSQL, and MySQL are some of the supported types. Then, available in public sever are the transforms that are contained in the commercial TAS.

Launching Maltego

For anyone to start maltego, you will go to the applications and look for backtrack. From there, you will get the information gathering and then to the network analysis where you will then see DNS analysis. From there, you will get into maltego. You will be prompted to register your product if you are accessing it for the first time. You will only need to input your email address and password if you have registered an account already. It will update the transforms when you have validated your login.

Hit on the tab 'investigate' after the updates of the transforms, and from the palette; you can choose your desired option. In the palette, you will see two major categories, which are personal and infrastructure. Also, other entities can be imported into the palette, for example, the Shodan entity. With the aid of their banner, you can find specific switches, routers, servers, and so on through a search engine like Shodan.

Web Scraping with Python

Let's assume you want to quickly pull a huge quantity of data from websites as fast as possible, how can you accomplish this feat without getting your data by going to each website at a time? Well, the short answer is web scraping. For what you intend to do to be faster and easier, you may want to result to web scraping. If you want to collect data from websites and when the volume is huge, you can use web scraping. However, what can instigate someone to want to collect massive data from sites? It is essential to discuss the web scraping application for us to understand the reason:

- **Job listings**: some details from websites regarding interviews, job openings, and so on, which users can easily access since it is listed in one place.
- **Development and research:** they collect temperature, general information, statistics, and so on from websites, which are a large set of information by using web scraping, and they use the result for R&D or to carry out surveys after analyzing it.
- **Social media scraping:** finding out what is trending by collecting data from social media websites like Twitter through web scraping.
- **Gathering email address:** web scraping is used by several organizations that use email marketing to send bulk emails after collecting them.
- **Price comparison:** for the comparison of the prices of products, web scraping is used by services like ParseHub to obtain information from online shopping sites.

The extraction of a massive quantity of information from websites is a technique of web scraping. The website's data are not structured, and to have it is a structured form, these unstructured data are collected by web scraping to do the job. Writing code, APIs, and online services are some of the different ways to scrape websites. Web scraping is allowed by some websites, while others don't allow it if we want to shift to the legal side of it. You may want to look at the "robots.txt" file of the website for you to know if such a website allows web scraping or not.

Shodan and Censys

It is in the Internet of Things that we are now living. Starting from the street security cameras and traffic light management systems to home WiFi routers, things that are connected to the Internet are always in our encounter. And it is both on the web and the real world that we can find all of them because they have a connection. With Google helping to discover your sought-after data on the web, you can also find these connected devices with some special search engines.

Let's welcome Shodan and Censys!

Since it has been in existence for about 7 years now, for the Internet of Things, the foremost, as well as the first search engine, is shodan. The inspiration behind the name came from a highly villainous artificial intelligence named Shodan, who was the System Shock, the computer game series' main antagonist. Though it has the capability of wrecking harm, shodan in the real-world is not as relentless. However, you will want to know how the search engine works before we go on to the bad news.

Shodan is typically similar to someone that knocks on every

door that they see as they wander throughout the neighborhood. However, there is the whole world instead of some city or knocking on every IPv4 address. This person would have some information and will give it to you if you ask them about a specific part of the neighborhood or a specific type of doors. The person would tell you the number of the doors, the individuals who answer these doors, and their utterances. And about those Internet of Things, you can get their information from shodan, which includes whether there is a web interface you can use, their type, and how they are called. Through, relatively cheap, you will need to subscribe to you to use shodan because it is not completely free.

Except there are no locks on some doors, you may find nothing so weird about knocking on some doors. And for the bad guys to break in, it may not be possible for anyone. Some systems that use default passwords and logins, including IP cameras and unprotected routers, are the representations of these doors in the world of Internet of things. You will see yourself gaining complete access to the password and login when you have managed to figure out them after entering their web-interface. And because you can easily find these default information about passwords and logins on the manufacturers' website, everything is no longer rocket science. And if it has the support of an IP camera, you can control and even see everything if it is an IP camera. Also, you may alter the settings if it is a router. You can even use a scary voice to talk to the poor baby if it is a baby monitor. Everything is up to the standards of your morals.

Chapter 13: Kali Linux on Portable Devices Like Raspberry Pi

Though, it can be fun enough to test networks, spoof accounts, or crack WiFi passwords. However, you may need an easily portable rig if you intend to take the show on the road. And so, here come the Raspberry Pi and Kali Linux. They designed Kali Linux for network penetration testing as an operating system. For you to test for Bluetooth vulnerabilities, spoof networks, WiFi passwords cracking, and plenty of other things, you have the chance of running it on your laptop. You need to know that you can be charged with a felony and get yourself arrested for violating the Computer Security Act if you break into protected networks using this knowledge. You can only use this knowledge to play with networks you control, for your learning, or simply use it for good. Now, since we have talked extensively about Kali Linux, and for the sake of not repeating all that you have read before, our focus will be on how we will build our Raspberry Pi and the version we will use. So, let's get it done!

For you to use Raspberry Pi, they don't require a lot of power for you to use them as a credit sized, small computer. You will have a super-portable system testing device that you can easily take with you anywhere you go with the combination of Kali Linux and Raspberry Pi.

The Essentials

- For you to perform initial installation, you will need a desktop computer
- Get a portable, small wireless keyboard with touchpad that one side of a small bag can contain
- It tends to be quite useful if you are carrying the Raspberry Pi with you around. So, a case is fine but optional
- New version of point-to-this-screen is essential though with Raspberry Pi 2 or newer versions; it doesn't fit flush
- An 8 GB SD card
- A Wi-Fi card
- You will be fine with a few external 5V batteries that use a USB part built for smartphones. So, you need a pack of battery
- Model 2 or B/B+ of Raspberry Pi. Though to install Raspberry Pi 2, you will need some additional steps;

you may want to use the Model B+ if you don't wish to go through those steps.

•

Step 1: Installation of Kali on the Raspberry Pi

For the Raspberry Pi, downloading and installing the touch screen build for Kali Linux will be the first thing you will need to do. The installation process is quite typical of installing any other operating system for Raspberry Pi. Here is a quick way to go about it:

Installation of Kali to Windows SD Card

1. For your hardware, you will need to download the Kali Linux Raspberry Pi. You can grab the Pi 2 version for Raspberry Pi 2 and the TFT version for model B/B++. Inside it, you will unzip the img file. You will need to take note here because, for Raspberry Pi, you will have to download the standard version of Kali Linux if you're not using the touch screen display.
2. You will need to have the application (.exec file) unzipped within after downloading Win32DiskImager.
3. With the use of a card reader, you will then have your SD card inserted into the Windows computer.
4. Then, you will double-click on the application, Win32DiskImager.exe that you have just downloaded.

5. At the top right of the device, you will click on the drop-down menu to select from the list if the application doesn't automatically detect your SD card.

6. The Raspbian .img file that you have just downloaded can be found when you click on the folder icon of the file from the application's image section.

7. Win32DiskImager will work its magic as you wait for it after you have clicked the 'write' button. You can insert your card into your Raspberry Pi after you have safely ejected your SD card when it finishes.

Kali installation in OS X SD Card

1. For you to work with it on your hardware, you will firstly need to have Kali Linux Raspberry Pi image downloaded. You will take Pi 2 version for Raspberry Pi 2 and TFT version for model B/B++. The standard version of Kali Linux for the Raspberry Pi is essential to be downloaded if it is the screen display that you are using.

2. For your installed version of OS X, have the appropriate version selected as you unzip the application after you have downloaded RPi-sd card builder.

3. With the use of a card reader, have your SD card inserted into your Mac.

4. Then, you can have your RPi-sd card builder opened. There will be an instant prompt for you to select an image of Raspbian. The file that you have had downloaded earlier is all you will have to select.

5. Then, another prompt will inquire about the connection of your SD card. All that is required of you is to click on 'continue' since it is connected when you

inserted it earlier. Then, the options for SD card will be presented to you. It will be checked, and you won't see anything else on the list if you have only had one inserted. Click ok on the card you want to use if not.

6. Then, you will enter the password for administration and press enter.

7. If there is any ejection of the SD card, you will see yet another prompt. Since for the application to perform a direct copy, it needs to unmount; there's nothing weird about it. In the Finder, for your SD card not to be available any longer, you will need to double-click it. A word of caution here: NEVER remove it from your USB port. You can click continue when you are sure.

8. Your SD card prepping will finish by the RPi-sd card builder. Then, you can insert it into your Raspberry Pi unit after you have safely ejected it.

Step 2: the Display Hook-Up

The touch screen works perfectly with the general-purpose input/output, which the Raspberry Pi has. You will see how this works ideally because, in the corner, it is the set of pins on your Raspberry Pi. Click into the display of the Raspberry Pi.

Step 3: Have Everything Plugged in and Launch

At this stage, you will need to plug in everything through the attacked display. Have your Wi-Fi adapter plugged into the USB ports. After that, plug the Pi into your pack of batteries.

Here, you can experience a clunky and slow process for the startup. If it takes some time, don't panic. First, before the startup process of the boot, for a bit while, you will see a white screen. Finally, a login screen will greet you. For you to get your screen working, you may have to work through some form of setup if you are using a Raspberry Pi 2. You may simply have to go to the next step if it is the B+ that you are using. Mainly, to get the screen running, there may be some needed steps for the current Raspberry Pi 2. A white, sad screen will welcome you when you boot it up initially. However, getting the screen working is not too hard. Unfortunately, Pi attachment may not require an HDMI monitor or through this part, you may need access into SSH. Then, to boot up your Pi, simply connect either of those.

Step 4: Enable Wi-Fi as you Log in

For you to make use of the tools within Kali Linux, you will want to enable the Wi-Fi card as you log in. your Wi-Fi card will be recognized automatically by the Raspberry Pi. However, it is essential to get into your network. The user interface of Kali Linux then needs to be powered up in the first place. Finally, you must change your device's password before you engage in anything else. If you don't, your device can be controlled by another person with the hacking skills.

Chapter 14: MalDuino

MalDuino has the capabilities of keyboard injection as an arduino-powered USB device. At superhuman speed, MalDuino will act as a typing, keyboard commands when you power it. Anything is possible with MalDuino since you can alter the desktop wallpaper or gain a reverse shell. Also, MalDuino can work well for pranksters, hobbyists, and penetration testers. The best BadUSB experience is all that MalDuino aims to provide. And using open-source libraries, it is through the arduino IDE that they have MalDuino programmed when it comes to software. You can convert the script written in DuckyScript into the code MalDuino will understand. For them to program it simply like, they would an Arduino; this makes it possible for expert arduino tinkerers to program it as well as making it newbie-friendly. The two versions of MalDuino are Lite and Elite.

Elite

You can select the script you intend running from the card since this version has four DIP switches and a Micro-SD card reader, and it is quite bigger. Also, you can program the keystroke injection scripts that the Micro-SD card stored apart from burning the fireware only once. This process is in contrary to the Lite version, which, when you want to run a different script, it will need to be flashed. You can drop, repurpose, or reprogram all these features altogether because it is straight from the Arduino that they programmed the two MalDuinos. Although you may have a few pins to play around with, you can purchase one and simply prefer to use it as a usual Arduino. You will be prompted to participate in the crowd-funding campaign particularly with the freedom that it offers.

Lite

The Lite version contains a switch apart from the USB connector, and this version is quite small. You can choose between programming and running mode with the function of the switch and the indication that the script has finished running through a LED. With more than enough space for most scripts, on its 32KB of onboard memory, the Lite stores a script. You can use the script converter to convert the scripts to malduino-friendly code since you can use a text editor to write scripts. Then, with the Arduino IDE, you can as well upload a script. Using the switch at the back, you can toggle the Lite into ready mode after you have unplugged the MalDuino Lite. Then, you can start using it!

The Hardware

The board of the Elite version measures around 4.6 cm x 1.1

cm, roughly 1.8 in x 0.43 in, which you can use an old case for it. For the Micro-SD card and DIP switches, you may need to cut some holes for them. It may come to your realization that the firmware it ships with is likely some kind of QC test for the dips after you exercise some RTFM and play around with the switches. Depending on which switches are on, these features make the output of MalDuino the numbers 1 to 4.

The Setup

Your Arduino IDE must not only be installed but also up to date when you want to set up the MalDuino. Because they programmed the Elite as a 'Sparkfun Pro Micro" that runs at 8 MHz and 3.3 V, it will be required of you to install the Sparkfun boards and open up the board manager. Then, the online portal of the Malduino Script Converter is your next point to go since there so many purposes that it servers like:

- For you to import to the IDE, it auto-generates the Arduino project
- You will have the freedom of selecting the language of your keyboard layout
- Between the Elite and Lite version, you can convert scripts through it

You only need to have the MalDuino flashed once and then store new scripts using the Micro-SD card when it is in normal operation as you empty script to download the project or create a simple script for the Elite version.

The Software

For you to run a command, a quick shortcut will be the combination of the ALT-F2 since you are running Linux. As such, you can save a file to `1111.txt` after scripting that into a file. Then, for a file that corresponds to the recent dip switch state, the search will be on the Elite for the Micro-SD card if you power the dip switch 4 and 2. As such, there will be an attempt by the software on parsing the content and finding the file with the name 0101.txt, i.e., not the binary representation of the number 4 and 2 but in dip switch order 1,2,3, and 4. Then, there will be a quick flashing of the red LED when it finishes. It is possible that only command functioning accurately is the ALT-F2 combo, and nearly all commands worked. Thus, you won't get any run command window without ALT-F2.

Protecting Yourself From MalDuino

As keystroke injection tools, a wider family of USB devices, referred to as BadUSBs is MalDuino. They have the capability of doing several types of devilish things by taking advantage of keyboard input as a trusted method of interfacing with a computer. However, what are the measures you can take to guard yourself against MalDuino? You can mitigate or protect yourself from the dangers of BadUSB attacks with the following 3 ways:

Admin Rights Lockdown

It doesn't matter if you are concerned about BadUSB attack or you are not; doing this can be quite useful. If you want to make changes to the admin-level, you only have to provide the prompt of yes or no to make changes that require admin rights on Windows 10. Even if the person is the admin, you will see that it is wrong and silly to provide someone that level of control. Before handling the keys to the castle, you can change this with a registry level edit to make the operating system require your admin password.

Duckhunt

This technique is applicable on Windows. There is a small application on github that can run as a backdoor process. The rate at which your keys are typed is what it continually monitors. When it detects unusual typing speeds, it will block all HID. However, some of the first few characters of an attach can likely get through and that is the only downside of it.

Physical Protection

It is simply a catch-all solution, and it is quite vital not to allow unauthorized devices from being plugged into your system. You can invest in some port blocker devices to block all access to USB ports physically. You may have to look deeper in the case of critical infrastructure. All the same, you can prevent any attack by using it when you are out in public.

Chapter 15: Kismet

As a wireless intrusion detection framework, kismet is a wardriving tool, sniffer, device detector, and wireless network. While kismet functions in compliance with hardware such as RTLSDR as well as some specialized capture hardware, it also works with certain software-defined radio, Bluetooth interfaces, and Wi-Fi interfaces. To some extent and under the WSL framework, kismet also functions with Windows but works well with OS X and Linux. Kismet works with Bluetooth and Wi-Fi interfaces, as well as other hardware devices on Linux. The built-in Wi-Fi interfaces enable it to function on OS X and works with remote captures on Windows 10.

Watching the Activities of Wi-Fi User Using Kismet

With a sight's direct line and directional Wi-Fi antenna, it is possible to detect the signals of Wi-fi passing through the walls of your home, even with its walls of privacy. People can learn a huge amount of data from this information, such as nearby devices' manufacturers, the movements of the residents, and also the network they use at a given time. For fixed targets, using kismet in a fixed situation can result in more nuanced information. Thus, it is ideal at displaying relationships between devices over time instead of just looking for the access point out there. The draw is from signal intelligence methods when we spy on users using kismet, whereby it is through the signals it conveys that we hope to learn about what we can't see. Here, Wi-Fi is the things we are dealing with and the devices that someone owns, human activity, connected devices, and routers are the things we are trying to see. Doing this goes a long way to your imagination. You will be more inclined to put off your Wi-Fi on unused devices and make a switch to a wired network if you are able to figure out that someone could see whether you were using your laptop or on your PlayStation and whether you were in your house. Using a wireless network, they use kismet to scan every available Wi-Fi channels silently by putting it in monitor mode for wireless packets for it to work its magic. You can see automated beacon frames as these packets that can be broadcasted by the wireless APs several times in a second. Also, not yet connected probe frames and data packets exchanged from connected devices. Kismet has the ability to visualize the activity of devices associated with specific networks as well as the networks themselves.

What We Can Get From Wi-Fi

So, how do we manage this situation? You can get on to explore nuanced details about a network you want to watch when you have identified it. You may want to look for details such as the network connection of the hardware and electronics of someone or an organization. You will be able to know the kind of configuration for some devices and also the recognition of various setups types for fingerprint. Not only will laptops and smartphones be plain to you, but you will also have the ability to see connected hydroponics or 3D printers with a setup such as this.

Now, the kind of person you are has a lot of dependence on the usefulness of this information. It would be useful to a thief who wants to discover expensive electronics by snooping around all homes in wireless range. Using a jamming attack, you can potentially target one or avoid one completely because wireless security cameras can be detected by kismet.

And when no one is in the house, we can easily infer since it's quite possible for us to see when the devices of clients use data, disappear, and appear. Also, with the use of the Wi-Fi signal data, hackers can combine data of the GPS by wardriving around a neighborhood. Doing this, each address of the wireless network will be possible for hackers when they build a map. Essentially, as there are already mapped networks by Google and Wigle Wifi, there could be an existence of this data. In the neighborhoods, for the detection of suspicious wireless activity, people can also use it as a neighborhood watch.

Essential Tools

There are some things needs to adhere to this guide. You will need kismet for you to run a Linux system, and for the scanning, you will also need a wireless network adapter that is compatible with Kali. Here, the older version which is stable is what we will discuss even though different wireless cards like macOS can run on the recent type of kismet. If your desire is to have it run on the Raspberry Pi, kismet will function perfectly on a Kali-Pi installation as well as a virtual machine.

Step 1: kismet installation:

The git repository will have to undergo a cloning process before the installation of kismet on Kali Linux. You may not need to worry about any dependencies based on the type of operating system that you are using. However, the slightly longer list of dependencies for kismet may be needed to be installed for smooth running of kismet. Since you will have to sort, login, decode, and detect a huge number of wireless data, they are quite needed. Also, you will need to install lots of libraries because you will be controlling a wireless card. Then, you will need to have the installation configured by navigating to the kismet directory. For your specific operating system distribution, this process will have the installation configured. Then, you can create the installation after the completion of that process. You will use the *suidinstall* option to complete the installation by running the resulting file with it. Then, you will install kismet. After the installation, you will need to capture packets as a non-root user by adding yourself to the kismet group. Ensure that your actual username is replaced in the space for "YourUsername."

Step 2: monitor-mode your wireless card:

With the USB settings, you will attach your wireless network card to the virtual machine or to your computer. The commands *ifconfig* or *ip a* can be used to find your card. You can use a "wlan0" or "wlan1" to name your card. You can then put your care in a monitor mode after naming it. At the end of the card's name, you will see a "mon" as it is renamed with this process. And to launch kismet, you will use this name.

Step 3: launch kismet:

It is simple to begin using kismet. For your card that you have put in wireless monitor mode, ensure to put the term after the −c since to specify the source it captures, kismet makes use of the −c. Then, kismet will start capturing packets after starting up. Then, you can return to the menu and make some customizations.

Several Wi-Fi devices that you can detect nearby will appear before you as you start kismet. Based on whether you are using 5 GHz, 2.4 GHz, or the two of them, you will have variance in the number of devices that you can detect.

Chapter 16: Bypassing a Hidden SSH

Now we need to take some time to look at going through and bypassing one of the SSH logins. We are going to do this by adding our own key to a remote server and then getting the access that we want. So if we want to go through and setup the SSH keys so that we can quickly and efficiently log in without a password, we are able to do this with a single command. This is going to be a simple process to go through.

The SSH is going to be known as the Secure Shell, and it is going to be a cryptographic network protocol that is going to be useful for helping us to operate the network services securely over a network that is unsecured. The typical applications that we are going to see with this one are going to include options like logging in with the command line and remote command execution, but it is possible that any network that you want to use is going to be secured with the SSH protocol.

The first step in this process is to make sure that we have been able to run the keygen command in order to generate the keys. If you have already generated some of these keys, then we are able to skip these steps. The code that we are able to use for this one is below

ssh -keygen -t rsa

Then we are able to go through and use this particular command in order to push the key so that it becomes connected to the remote server. This is going to be something that we are able to modify in order to match the user name of the server and the host name of your server as well. We will be able to go through and use the code below to make this happen.

cat ~/.ssh/id_rsa.pub | ssh user@hostname 'cat >> .ssh/authorized_keys'

The first time that we copy over these keys, we are going to need to enter the password to help the program get set up and ready to go. After that first time, though, we should be able to login without needing a password, or even use the rsync or scp without entering the password at all. You are able to test this iwt the following command:

ssh user@hostname

It is definitely going to be a lot easier to go through compared to typing in a password all of the time.

Nd, that is all that we need to do. It is going to spend some time helping us to get onto the SSH and will make it easier for us to get onto this without needing to use a password each time that we do the work. Getting this done can be hard, and you do need to know the password the first time around, but if you are able to get ahold of this, and you will be able to get onto the network any time that you would like.

Chapter 17: Bypassing a Mac Address Authentication and Open Authentication

Another thing that we are able to do when it comes to hacking is to bypass the Mac Address Authentication in order to get onto the network that we want to use. This is going to be a feature that we are going to find with Mac addresses that will allow us to get onto the system and use it in the manner that we would like. This will ensure that we are able to either get onto our network when it is not working well or on another option that we would like to use, such as hacking into another computer. Let's take a look at how this is going to work.

The Media Access Control address, or the MAC address, is going to be interesting because it is able to uniquely identify each node that is going to show up in a network. It is going to take the form of six pairs of hexadecimal digits, which can include 0 to 9, and all of the letters A to F, that are going to be separated out by either dashes or colons.

This MAC address is usually going to be associated with the network adaptor or a device that has some networking capabilities. Because of this reason, it is going to be known in many cases as the physical address. The first three pairs of these digits in the address are going to be called the Organizational Unique Identifier, and we need to take some time to look at them because they help us to identify the company that either sold or manufactured the device. Then the last three pairs of digits that are going to show up are going to be the specific numbers that just go to that device, and can be like the serial number of the whole process.

With this in mind, we are going to spend some time going through and looking at some of the steps that we need to use in order to bypass the MAC address filtering on some of our wireless networks. The first step that we need to work with is considering that we are going to working with a router that has the MAC Filtering Configured in the first place. We can say that our MAC address is going to be AA-BB-OO-11-22. This is one that is allowed to show up when we are using the MAC filtering on our own wireless network.

Then it is time to move on. We can log into the machine that we are using for Kali Linux and then put that Wi-Fi adapter into the mode that allows it to monitor what is going on around it. This is going to be done with the airmon-ng and can be done with the simple command into our terminal below:

Airmon-ng start wlan()

Now it is possible that some of the processes with Kali Linux when you do this will show us some errors. If you do end up with some issues or an error message here, then you need to kill the process in this program that seems to be having the issue. You are able to do this with the command below:

Kill [pid]

Now it is time to go through and launch another part of this process, which is the Airodum-ng. This will help us to locate the wireless network that we want to work with, and will even help us to see which clients are connected in this whole process. The command that we are able to use to make this one happen is below:

airodump-ng –c [channel] –bssid [target router MAC Address] –i wlanomon

This should then show us a whole list of the clients who are connected to this device at the bottom of our terminal. Then the second column is going to list the MAC addresses of all the connected clients we will be able to spoof at this time in order to get that wireless networked authenticated so we can do what we would like on it.

The one thing to note at this time is that you are only going to get a list with this step if there is actually someone who is connected to the wireless network that we are looking at. If you do not have someone currently connected to the device, then you will not get a list at this point.

Now it is time for us to go on to the next step. After having been able to go through and find the MAC address that you want to use, it is time to go through the process of using the MacChange rin order to spoof the MAC address that we want to work with. We are going to spend our time spoofing the MAC address of your wireless adapter, but the first thing that we need to do here before we get started, we need to take down the interface for monitoring known as wlanomon and wlano. This is going to allow us to make some of the changes that we want to the MAC address. We are able to do this with the following command to make things a little easier:

Airmon-ng stop wlanomon

When that process is done, we are able to take down the wireless interface who's MAC address we want to spoof in the following command:

Ifconfig wlano down

Then this is going to bring us the MacChanger. We are able to use this tool in order to change up the MAC address. The code that we are able to do with this one will be below:

Macchanger -m [New MAC Address] wlano

And then we want to go through and bring all of that back up. Remember, a few steps above, we went through and closed down the system so that we could change ours and get ourselves on this option. But now we want to go through and bring it all back up again. The code that we are able to work with here will include:

Ifconfig wlano up

Now that we have been able to change up the MAC address that is on our wireless adapter to a white listed MAC address that the other network will allow, we are able to try out authenticating with the network and see whether this worked and if we are able to connect to the process as well.

And that is all there is to get this done. Keep in mind that this process can take a bit of time if you are not going to find someone who is on the network right in the beginning. You may need to have some patience with this one to make sure that it is going to work the way that you would like and to ensure that you can actually find the right MAC address that is going to work with that router.

But once you have been able to go through and change up your MAC address so that it works well with one of the other options that belong to that wireless network so that you are able to get on as well. This is a simple process is going to be able to help us learn more about the process and how we are able to work with getting onto the network that we would like along the way.

Chapter 18: Hacking WPA and WPA2

The world of wireless networks is going to be great for a lot of consumers. It adds on a lot of protection to the networks of the past, and it is going to be important to helping us to work with our wireless network while on the move and without having to be connected to your cable all of the time. The WPA and WPA2 options are going to be some of the best when it comes to keeping your information safe, but it is possible for hackers to get onto them if they are patient, and they are ready to go through and take on the hard work. That is why we are going to spend some time in this chapter taking a look at the steps that are necessary to hack onto these two wireless networks.

The first thing that we need to take a look at is preparing our attack. We need to first have a better understanding of when we are able to legally hack into a Wi-Fi network. In most regions, the only time that you are able to legally hack onto some of these networks is when the network belongs to you, or if it belongs to someone who has given us written permission to hack into the network so that you can check it and make sure that it is safe from a hacker. Hacking networks that don't meet the criteria that are above, then the hacking process is illegal and it could be known as a federal crime if you are caught in the act.

Now that this is out of the way, it is time for us to go through and download the disk image of Kali Linux. This is going to be one of the preferred tools to work with when it is time to hack these networks. You can download the installation image, also known as the ISO, by using the following steps:

1. The first step that we will work with is to go to the https://www.kali.org/downloads/ on the web browser of your needs.
2. Click HTTP next to any of the versions of this that you would like to use.
3. Wait for the file to finish with the downloading process.

From here, we want to be able to attach a flash drive over to the computer that we are working with. The flash drive that we are using is required to come with 4 gigabytes of space or higher in order to complete this process. Then we can make the flash drive bootabe. Finish up the rest of the steps that you need to do to get the Kali Linux system set up and ready to go on your own computer.

When the Kali Linux system is set up and ready, it is time to begin the actual hack that we want to accomplish. We can do this by opening up the terminal for Kali Linux on your computer. You can find and click on this Terminal app icon, which is going to look like a black box that has a white ">_" on it. You can also just click on Alt, Ctrl, T to open this terminal up.

This is the time where you will want to install Aircrack to help with the attack. You are able to type in the command that is below to help you get this one started:

sudo apt-get install aircrack-ng

When the prompt comes up for this one, you will want to enter in the password. You can type in the password you use to log into that computer in the first place. Then press on the Enter button. This is going to make sure that the root access is going to be enabled for any of the other commands that you would like to be able to execute in the Terminal. If you decide at this time to open up another window for a Terminal, which is possible, remember that you may have to go through and run a command with the sudo prefix or choose to enter the password into the system again to get the best results.

This is where we are going to be able to install the Aircrack-ng program that we were talking about before. When it prompts you to, you should press on Y, then wait until the program has time to finish installing overall. When this installation is done, it is time to turn on the airmon-ng. type in the command to do this and then press on Enter to continue.

Then it is time for us to go through and find the name of the monitor that we want to use. You are going to find this located somewhere in the Interface column. If you are working to do this attack on your own network, then it is going to be named as wlan0. If you do not see the name of the monitor at all, then be aware that your specific card for Wi-Fi is not going to support this kind of monitoring at all.

Now it is time for us to go through and start the process of monitoring our network. You are able to do this with the following command below, and then press enter when you are done

Airmon-ng start wlano.

Make sure that you press the right name of the network that you would like to monitor. If you are doing your own, then you would add in the wlano. But if you are trying to monitor the wireless of another computer, then you will need to make some changes in order to handle this and make sure that you are actually managing the different network that you would like.

Then we need to go through and enable a monitor mode interface with this. When we find that, we are able to enter the following command to help us get this set up:

Iwconfig

Now, there could be a few different processes that show up, and it is possible that some of them are going to return errors to us. If this happens, then we will want to kill any of the processes that are going to return errors to us. This is often going to happen when the Wi-Fi card is going to conflict with some of the running services on your computer. You are able to kill these processes when you go through and use the command below:

Airmon-ng check kill

While we are here, we want to review the name of the monitor interface. In most cases, the name is going to be something that is pretty simple, like mono or wlanomon. We also want to make sure to tell the computer that it is time to listen to some of the nearby routers. To get a list of the routers that happen to be in the same range as you, you are able to enter the command below:

Airodump-ng mono

Make that you replace the mono with the right part. We want to have it filled in as the name of the monitor interface that we used in the previous step, or this is not going to work the way that we would like.

As you are searching around, we need to make sure that we are doing some searching here. We need to be able to find the router that we would most like to hack. At the end of each string of text that comes your way, you are going to see a name. You want to look through this to find the one that belongs to the network that you would most like to hack into in the process.

During this process, we need to make sure that we are working with the right router, and that we are choosing one that comes with WPA or WPA2 security that is attached back to it. If you see one of these on the left of the name of the network, then it is time to proceed. Otherwise, this is not going to be a network that you are able to hack along the way.

This is where we are going to be able to note the MAC address and the channel number of the router that we want to work with. These are going to be the pieces of information that we should notice on the left of the name of the network. The MAC address is going to be the line of numbers that we are going to find on the far-left side of the line for the router. On the other hand, the channel is going to be a number of some sort that is found to the left of the tag that you have for the WPA or WPA2.

In this part, we are going to be able to monitor the selected network until we see a handshake. This is going to occur when an item connects to a network, or when the computer is able to connect to a router. Enter in the code below in order to make sure that we are replacing the components that are necessary of the command with the information on the network:

Airodum-ng -c channel —bssid MAC -w /root/Desktop/ mono

In this one, there are going to be a few things that are going to happen. First, we are able to replace the channel with the channel number that we were able to find in the other step.

Then we want to replace MAC with the MAC address that we plan to us or spy on here.

Remember that we also need to go through and replace the mono with whatever the name of the interface is that you want to work with.

When this is all in place, we just wait around for some time to see that handshake appears. Once you see a line that has the tag of WPA handshake, and it is followed with a MAC address that shows up at the top of your screen on the right, then it is time to proceed. It is also possible for us to move this along and not wait around all of the time, it is possible for us to force a handshake using the deauth attack before we continue on with this part.

When it is time to go through and get that handshake, then you will be able to get onto the network and look at what is going on, as long as the other person does not have the proper security on their network at that time. You will then be able to get through some of the security protocols that are there, and this allows you to look around, read through and change some of the packets that are shown, and so much more. You need to work with a few tools to make this happen, but it can be a successful method to finish the hack that you would like to accomplish.

Chapter 19: Secure and Anonymous Using Tor, Proxy Chains, and VPN

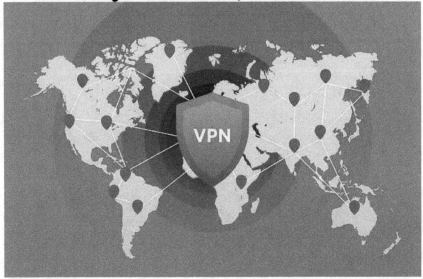

There are going to be some situations where you would like to get onto a network and do some of the work that you want, without other people being able to track where you are going. Being secure and anonymous online is something that a lot of people aim for in their work, and it is sometimes hard to make sure that you can get to this point, and maintain that secrecy. That is why we are going to spend some time looking at the different methods that we are able to use to keep ourselves hidden and safe when we are online.

What is Tor

Tor is going to be a protocol for internet networking that has been designed in order to anonymize the data that is relayed across it. Using this software is going to make it, at a minimum, hard, if not impossible, for snoops to come onto the network and see your social media posts search history, webmail and other online activity that you try to do. They will also find that it is hard to figure out what country you are from, just by analyzing your IP address. This can be useful for a lot of people who want to be online.

When you run this service, some of the bigger data collectors, like Google Ads and other options will not be able to go through and perform some of the traffic analysis that they want, and they will not be able to go through and gather up some data on the habits that you are doing online. This also makes it harder for hackers to gather that information as well.

The Tor network is interesting in that it is going to run through the servers of thousands of volunteers who are found through the world. The data that you use is going to be bundled up in packets that are encrypted when they enter into this network. Then, unlike how we see with our traditional internet connections, Tor is going to be able to strip away part of the header of the packet, which is going to be part of the addressing information that can be used to help us learn some things about the sender, such as the operating system where this message was originally sent from.

Finally, Tor is going to be able to encrypt the rest of the information that we use for addressing, called the packet wrapper. This is something that the regular connections that we use with the internet are not going to use this. Then our data packets, which are encrypted and modified, will be routed through many of these volunteer servers, known as relays, while it makes its way to the final destination. The roundabout way that these packets are going to travel on this network is going to make it harder to track.

Each of the relay parts is going to decrypt just enough of that wrapper to know which relay the data came from in the first place, and which relay it needs to send that packet to the net. The relay is then able to rewrap this in a new wrapper before sending it along again.

While this method is not 100 percent accurate all of the time, it is going to be able to keep your information a lot safer than we will see with regular connections to the internet. The fact that we are encrypting the data that we use, and that we are able to work with this in a manner that relies on relays rather than sending it just one place at a time, can make it a lot easier and more secure to work with.

Using Proxy Chains

Another option that we are able to work with here to ensure that our information is going to stay safe and secure along the way is to work with these proxy chains. These are going to make it a lot harder for the hacker to find us and what we are doing. It will utilize an intermediary machine whose IP address is going to be the one left on the other system, rather than our own. And the Proxy system is set up to make this all work.

The proxy chain is going to be used to help us to accept our own traffic, and then we will forward it on to the target that should receive it. The proxy is going to spend time logging all of the traffic that we would like to send in either direction, but the good news is that if someone would like to look through this log, they would need to get a search warrant or a subpoena to do it, and this makes it harder for us to get onto the other network without anyone finding us.

If we are able to take some of our coding skills and string more than one of these proxies into a chain, it is going to become even more difficult for the other computer to detect the original IP address that we want to work with. On the other hand, if one of the proxies is found to be out of the jurisdiction of the victim, then it is going to be really unlikely that any traffic is going to actually come back to our own IP address.

The good news is that, if you would like to stay hidden with the help of proxies, both BackTrack and Kali with Linux are going to have some good tools that are going to help with doing this process, and this is going to be known as a proxy chain. It is up to you to determine if this is the right option to keep your network secret and hidden.

VPNs

Another tool that we are able to work with when it is time to keep our network safe is the VPN. This is going to stand for a Virtual Private Network, and it is going to allow you a way to create a secure connection to another network through the internet. These can be a great option to use in some cases when we would like to access websites that are restricted based on your region, to help your browsing activity from others seeing it, and more.

These VPNs are really popular though they are not going to be used in many cases for the original purpose for what they were designed for. They were originally made to help connect a business network together over the internet or allow you a way to access a business network when we are at home.

To keep this as simple as possible, the VPN is going to be able to connect your computer, tablet, or smartphone to another computer or another server somewhere on the internet, and you are able to browse the internet with that connection to keep things safe. So, if you see that this server is found in another country, it is going to seem as if you are actually in that company and allows us to pull up information and services that we would normally never be able to gain access to at all.

There are a lot of great ways that we are able to benefit when it comes to working on the VPN. These are going to include:

1. Will help us to bypass some of the restrictions on location when it comes to websites or streaming some of the video and audio that we would like to get ahold of.
2. It can make it easier to stream some of the content that we would like on Hulu and Netflix.
3. Will make it easier to protect yourself from thins like snooping or issues with hotspots of Wi-Fi so that it is harder for a hacker to gain the access that they want.

4. Will help us to gain at least a little bit of anonymity when we are online and can really hide our true location from others.
5. Makes it easier to protecting yourself from being logged when you are torrenting.

It is common for people to work with VPN and other services when they would like to bypass some of the geographic restrictions to watch the shows and movies that they would like in different countries or even to help with torrenting. This can be especially useful when you would like to hack, though, because it makes it harder for others to find you and figure out where all of the attacks are coming from in the first place.

Chapter 20: IP Spoofing

The next topic that we need to spend a bit of time on here is the idea of IP spoofing. This is going to be a process where we are able to create packets for the Internet Protocol that are going to have modified source addresses in them, to either help us hide the identity of the person who is sending the information, to help us to impersonate another system of computers, and sometimes for both. This is often going to be the technique that a hacker is going to use when they would like to perform a DDoS attack against their target device or against the surrounding infrastructure.

Sending and receiving these packets is going to be one of the main methods that these networked computers and devices are going to communicate, and it is going to be kind of the basis of how the modern internet is going to work. All of these IP packets are going to come with a header, which is then going to be followed by the body of the packet, and will contain some of the important information on routing like the source address. In a normal packet, one that the hacker has not messed around with, the source IP address is simply going to be the address of who sent the packet. But if the hacker has been able to spoof the packet, then the address is going to be forged instead.

IP spoofing is going to be analogous to an attacker sending out a package to someone with the wrong address to return listed out. If the person who received the package wants to stop the sender from sending out this package, blocking all of the packages that come from that address is not going to do much good because the return address can be changed as well.

Along the same idea here, if the receiver would like to be able to respond to the return address that they see on the packet, their response package is going to not head to the real sender. Instead, it is going to head to whichever IP address that the hacker stole to use. The ability to spoof the addresses of packets is going to be one of the biggest vulnerabilities that we are going to see with these DDoS attacks.

For example, the DDoS attack is going to be reliant on spoofing with the goal of overwhelming a target with traffic while masking the identity of the source that comes with it. This is going to make it harder to work with any mitigating efforts if the IP address of the source is false, and it is randomized on a continuous basis, blacking the requests that are malicious are going to be a lot harder to do. IP spoofing, as a result, is going to make it really hard for cyber security teams and law enforcement to track down who is causing the attack.

Along the same lines, we are going to find that spoofing is also going to be used to help us masquerade as another device when we would like. So that the responses that come with this are going to be sent over to the device that we are targeting instead of over to us. Some attacks, including the volumetric attacks like DNS amplification, are going to rely on this kind of vulnerability. The ability that we have in order to modify the source IP is going to be a big part of the design that we are going to see with the TCP/IP protocol, which means that we are always going to have to be worried about what is happening here.

Tangential to the DDoS attacks that we talked about before, spoofing is going to be done with the whole aim of hiding and pretending to be another device. This is going to allow the hacker to come in and sidestep the authentication and to gain access to or hijack the session of another user. The hacker is then able to go through the process of doing whatever they would like with this network, which is going to allow them to cause some damage and attack the network, without anyone being able to attach it back to them.

Chapter 21: Penetration Testing with Metasploit

The final thing that we are going to take a look at here is how to work on a penetration test, and how we are able to use the Metasploit system to help us get all of this done. Penetration testing, or a pen test, is going to be a process that involves attacking some of the information systems in a similar way as an attacker would to your system. This helps us to find some of the vulnerabilities in the system and close them up before the hacker can get to them.

The distinguishing characteristic that we are going to find with pen testing is that there will not be any harm done to the system, and the owner of that system will provide the necessary consent before you get started. The vulnerability that we will see will be defined as a weakness in the security that is going to exist in a part of our system that will provide an entry point for the hacker to use to start their attack. There are a number of places where these vulnerabilities are going to show up, such as errors in the design, bugs, and more.

Some of the most common entry points for these attacks and places where we need to check out before a hacker can get to them includes the browsers, SQL injection, flash, ActiveX, and social engineering.

Due to the different scenarios that can cause an attack, different penetration testing types are going to be needed. The three types of testing that we are able to look through can include white box, black box, and gray box testing. When we start out with some of the black box testing, then none of the information about that system is going to be provided back to the person who is doing the testing. It is going to be the responsibility of our tester in order to gather up the right information about the system that they are supposed to attack.

Then we are able to move on to the white box testing. This helps because it is going to provide complete information about the target system from the beginning. This is going to be useful because it helps us to understand some of the impacts that can happen with an internal attack on the network.

And then we finally have the grey box attack. This is going to be where the tester is going to get some of the information about this system, but not all of it. These tests are going to be the most useful to help us better understand what can happen, and the main impact, of one of these external attacks.

So, we need to work through the four stages that are going to happen when we work with penetration testing and the Metasploit process. The first stage that we are going to focus on is the planning out the test that we want to use. The objective of this is to help us to identify the scope and even the strategy that we want to use in order to carry out this test. The scope of this test is going to be informed by currently practiced policies and standards.

The second stage that we are able to work with is going to be known as discovery. There are going to be three things that we are able to do here. The first one is to gather up some of the information on the system and some of the data that it holds. This is going to be known as fingerprinting. Then we reach the second activity and that is known as scanning and even probing system ports. And finally, the third activity is going to help us to identify any vulnerabilities that the system is going to have.

The third stage of this testing is going to be all about the attack. This stage is going to be able to help us identify the exploits for the vulnerabilities. An exploit is going to be a computer program that has the objective of utilizing a vulnerability in order to get the necessary access to that system overall. after the hacker is able to gain this access, the payload is going to be the software that will help them to gain the necessary control over that compromised system. The exploit is going to be done in order to help deliver the payload that we are working with here.

And then we end up with the fourth stage. This is one that can often be forgotten, but if you are doing this process for someone else, then you will want to pay attention to it to help them out. This stage is going to be known as reporting. The objective that we are going to see with this stage is that it helps us to create a detailed report of some of the identified vulnerabilities of the system, the impact that they have on our business, and some of the necessary solutions.

Although there are going to be a ton of different tools that are able to help out with this process, Metasploit is going to be one of the tools that is used the most. That is why we are going to spend some time looking at how to do this kind of process, the process of working with a penetration testing, and how it can be done with Metasploit.

First, we have to realize that Metasploit is going to be a framework that has been organized into modules. The first type is going to be to do the exploit. These types of modules are designed in a manner so that they are able to take advantage of any weaknesses that are found in a system. These are going to be things like code injection, application exploits, and buffer overflow.

Then there are going to be some of the auxiliary modules. These are going to be the ones that will perform some actions, but these actions are not set up to take direct advantage of some of the weaknesses on the system. For example, these can be things like service denial and scanning.

The third type of module that is found on this system is going to be the post-exploitation modules. These are important as well because their main focus is going to be helping us gather information on some of the target systems.

And finally, we are going to find the payload modules. These are going to be the modules that can run after a weakness has been exploited in a successful manner. The payload is going to provide the means to help us control the system that w were able to exploit along the way. With this payload, it is easier to open up the meterpreter to help write out the DLL files.

So now, we need to take a moment to download this system to get it up and running. We are going to go through and do it with the Windows installation here, but you are able to go through and make changes and do some of the work that you would like to prevent other issues along the way as well, and it will work in a similar manner on other systems. You just need to go to the Metasploit website and then click that you want to do the Windows installation.

From here, you will want to download the installer, and then there will be some prompts that show up that will help you to get this installation completed. To help confirm that the installation was a success, you need to start the command prompt, making sure that you are the administrator, and then use the command of "commanmsfvenom.bat -helpd." If you get an output, then this will show you that it worked, and it should list out all of the different options that are available for you to use from this part.

There are a few options that we are able to work with here. For example, if we would like to be able to list out all of the payloads that are available, we would be able to work with the command of "msfvenom.bat -list payloads." This could be a long list, but it still shows us what is available here.

If you would like to go through and start up the console that is available with Metasploit, you will need to use the command of msfconsole.bat. You will then be able to access the msf console, which is going to be the tool that we can use for the command line that is going to work with this program.

The next thing on the list that we are able to focus on, we need to list out all of the exploits that we have available with the help of the command help search. If we want to go through and search around for a specific exploit, you will need to use the CVE number, platform, or name. Let's say that we want to be able to list out all of the exploits that happened in the year of 2018. To do this, we would need to bring out the command of "search cve:2018" and this should list out all of the parts that we need.

To go through this process and then gather up some of the information about the exploit that happened, we need to pass the url of that exploit and make sure that it is in the info command. The code that we are able to work with to make this happen includes:

Exploit/multi/browser/java_jre17_exec.

After we are able to look through the list and then we can find an interesting exploit that we want to use, it is time to use the command that we used above. After we issue the command that we want to work with that specific exploit, it is possible for us to set some of the options that we want to use with the set command. This could be something like setting the local port and local host. The commands that we are able to use to make this one is going to happen will include the following:

set SRVHOST 0.0.0.0
set SRVHOST 8080

If you would like to be able to go through and check the variables that we are able to set, we would want to work with the command, show options to get it done. When the exploit that we are working with has more than one target, we are able to set a specific target by specifying an ID to the set target command. Some of the available targets that we will want to work with are going to be listed with the help of the command of show targets.

Working with the Metasploit program is going to make it a lot easier for us to go through and complete one of our own penetration tests. This is going to make it easier for us to go through and learn a bit more about our system, and figure out where some of the most common vulnerabilities are going to show up and how we are able to close them up and keep the hackers out.

Conclusion

Thank you for making it through to the end of *Hacking with Kali Linux*, let's hope it was informative and able to provide you with all of the tools you need to achieve your goals whatever they may be.

The next step is to get to be where we are able to spend a bit of time learning more about the world of hacking and how we are able to utilize it for some of our own needs. Whether you are looking to protect your own network and make sure that a hacker is not able to get onto the system, or you are more interested in hacking onto another network and taking the information (which, as we discussed, is illegal), you can utilize a lot of the techniques and other methods that are found in this guidebook.

There are a lot of different parts that come together when we are trying to work with hacking, and Kali Linux is going to be a great resource to help us get through some of these hacking, and will ensure that we are able to get this all done. We spent some time taking a look at how to set up the Kali Linux system so that it is ready to go and help us with all of the hacking that we want to do along the way.

In addition to being able to work with the Kali Linux system in order to get some of our hacking done, we also need to spend some time taking a look at some of the other hacking techniques that we are able to use. We are going to spend some time looking at how to do a penetration test, some of the man in the middle attacks, denial of service attacks, how to get onto some of the wireless networks, and the importance of a penetration test.

Then we took some time to look at the different parts that are able to help us to keep our networks safe. For example, with the help of a good firewall and the use of penetration testing, and even VPN's and other options like this to keep your anonymity when you are online, you will be able to make it a bit harder for the hacker to find you, and this makes it so much easier for you to keep all of that information as safe as possible.

There are many parts that come to the world of hacking, and it is important that we learn some of the methods and techniques that come with this in order to keep things organized and to keep the hackers out. When you are ready to learn a bit more about hacking and how it can work for some of our needs, make sure to check out this guidebook to help you to get started.

www.ingramcontent.com/pod-product-compliance
Lightning Source LLC
LaVergne TN
LVHW051221050326
832903LV00028B/2196